Astrology
for the New Age

An Intuitive Approach

by Marcus Allen

Whatever Publishing
Berkeley, California

Published by Whatever Publishing
PO Box 3073, Berkeley CA 94703

Designed by Marcus Allen
Cover photo by Dean Campbell
Calligraphy by Stephanie Young
Artwork by Rainbow Canyon

Manufactured in the United States of America

Library of Congress Cataloging in Publication Data

Donicht, Mark.
    Astrology for the new age.

    1. Astrology. I. Title.
BF1708.1.D66   1979   133.5   79-10433
ISBN 0-931432-03-0

*Dedicated to the children
of the New Age*

Special thanks to
    Mac Pierce for his three-day crash course in astrology when we first drove out to California;
    Joel Schwartz for teaching me how to cast charts;
    Lee Duvlea for showing me a simple method of casting charts;
    David Lueck for his Aquarian interpretations;
    Abraham for his planetary walks and his enthusiasm;
    Lama Tarthang Tulku for his penetrating mind and interest in astrology;
    Shakti Gawain for her support and encouragement —and for giving me space when I need it;
    my spirit guide for his insight and clarity and presence.

A Word....

I hope in this book to accomplish for astrology what I feel Eden Gray accomplished for the tarot in her beautiful book, *The Tarot Revealed*: I wish to provide even complete beginners with enough information and guidance so that they can skillfully use the tools of this ancient, deep teaching, and make them their own in a very short time.

And even more: I pray we can discover meaningful tools for not only transforming our own lives, but bringing about the transformation of the entire planet as well. I intend to keep revising this book, if necessary, until these goals are reached.

Your feedback is deeply appreciated. Write me in care of the publisher.

Be in peace

Marcus

Divine Master,
be my guide
be my light
be my voice
May your words of truth
flow thru this vessel
May your words of truth
speak thru me
Divine Master,
be my guide
be my light
be my voice

Foreword

Astrology at the dawn of a New Age — *an intuitive approach*.

New discoveries are transforming our thinking, transforming our consciousness... Our rational, linear approach has finally discovered that there are other approaches to knowledge — other ways to learn and grow... A change of consciousness is taking place on a mass scale, in which intuitive channels are opening —

> *"Your old people will see visions,*
> *and your children will dream dreams."*

This book does not have to be used in a linear way.

Each section is in some ways complete in itself. Just absorb as much of any part of it as you wish. This is a different approach to astrology than most — an intuitive approach, which tries to involve rational mind information as little as possible, and open up direct, intuitive channels as much as possible...

Don't try to absorb all of the information in this book at once. Just take part of it, and sit with it, letting it open up as much within you as possible ... letting as many images, free associations, memories surface as possible...

This book presents several different keys — keys for understanding astrology as a whole. Sit with each of them. Relax. There is far more information within each of us — deep storehouses of intuitive information and understanding — than we can comprehend with our rational minds. And all we need to do to connect with this information is to relax and let it surface.

The truth is within you.

Contents

A Note About the Style

I use dots or periods in an unusual way . . . Most of us read too fast, I feel — the dots are an attempt to encourage you to slow down . . . Every time you come to three dots, pause . . . take a breath . . . let the words sink in . . .

Take your time . . . you're in no hurry . . . This is not intended to be a book for practicing your speed reading.

Relax, and enjoy!

Preface

In the tradition which has now come to us from the mystical land of Tibet, it is told that Manjushri, the embodiment of wisdom, gave the science and artform of astrology to the people of ancient times as a tool to aid their understanding.

But the people misused astrology — it became a limiting game, a pastime in itself, rather than a tool for *dharma*, for 'words of truth', for growth and understanding, going beyond all limitations. So, Manjushri took the astrology books away from the people, and hid them in a cave, until such time that the people would be ready to use the teachings skillfully and meaningfully . . .

Then, much later, a man named Padma Sambhava (meaning "the Lotus Born") entered into Tibetan history. Padma Sambhava is the great teacher and skilled magician, the father of Tantra who brought the Vajrayana — Tantric Buddhism — into Tibet in the 8th century A.D.

Padma Sambhava prayed deeply and powerfully to Manjushri, summoning him and asking for the astrology texts, praying that, this time, the people would be ready to use their knowledge for their own good. Manjushri granted his prayer, and told him where the texts were hidden. In this way, Padma Sambhava was able to re-introduce the ancient intuitive science of astrology to the people of Tibet.

And now, finally, at the dawn of a new age, Padma Sambhava's teachings have come to the West, just as the ways of the West have come to the East.

Now, finally, at the dawn of the Age of Aquarius, it is time to rediscover astrology again, to see within it a powerful, valuable tool to be used for deep inner growth, for the spreading of light and love thruout the world, thruout the galaxies, wherever we may wander.

An Introduction

Aquarian astrology at the dawn of a new age . . .

Astrology involves visualizing the solar system, and beyond . . .
It is an infinite series of cycles . . . cycles within cycles . . .

One of the most intriguing cycles which is charted in astrology is
the 'great movement' of the 'great age': the precession of the
equinox. Each full revolution thru all 12 signs takes 26,000 years
— 2166 years for each sign . . . (That's 72 years for each single
degree of the precession — the length of our lifetime.)

Right now, we are on the cusp of two of the deepest signs — we
are moving from the Age of Pisces into the Age of Aquarius.
Cusps are the deepest places of a chart: they are the places of
transformation, where one sign transforms into the next.

No one to my knowledge knows the exact beginning of the
Piscean Age, but everyone traces it at least to the time of Christ
2,000 years ago.

Pisces is the final, deepest sign . . . the sign of the end, of
completion of a cycle . . . of total, deep understanding . . .
absolute reality: absolute emptiness (*Shunyata* — shimmering
emptiness) . . . ruled by the energies of both Neptune, the
Visionary, and Pluto, the Beyond . . .

The Age of Pisces entered with the world crucifying its Christ, and it is coming to an end with the atom bomb and the possibility of global annihilation . . .

The Age of Aquarius is the age of the dawning light . . . the light of understanding. Aquarius is the Water-Bearer, nourishing and healing the earth with spiritual awareness . . . It is the Age influenced by the energy of the planet Uranus, which is the Enlightener, the inventor, the Awakener . . . It is erratic, spontaneous, unpredictable . . .

The Age of Aquarius is the time in which humankind once again clearly connects with higher intelligence, divine forces — the symbol of Aquarius is the Angel as well as the Water-Bearer . . .

New doors of perception are opened . . . new levels of consciousness are experienced . . . ancient truths re-emerge . . . intuitive sciences re-emerge . . . understanding beyond that of the rational mind is rediscovered . . . the head once more becomes united with the heart . . . humankind once more merges with its source, with its God, with its light — the deep truth of its deepest levels of being.

A Question

Why study astrology? What is the purpose of interpretation?

One good reason is because it's fun.

And another *very* good reason is that astrology can open us up intuitively . . . It can be a very useful tool for finding your path . . . seeing the face of God within you . . . and within others.

Each of the 12 signs has its own unique energy . . . its own skillful means . . . its own path . . . its own power. It's all part of the beauty and the bounty of the Universe. There are infinite possibilities — and these are reflected when we use a tool such as astrology . . . or Tarot, or Zen meditation, or music, or dance . . . or *whatever*.

Every chart is a Mandala — a complete cosmology in itself . . . a map of the entire Universe. The 'macrocosm-microcosm' teaching is brilliant, and very deep: *As above, so below. As below, so above.* Each little piece of the Universe is in its own way a complete Universe, reflecting the whole. In the atom, the galaxy is mirrored.

So we can, if we wish, look at a chart as a purely 'arbitrary' design, on a piece of paper, that we will sit with, and see what associations will arise . . . As we take this time to look, as we do this ritual, we start to see many things . . . Mirrors within mirrors . . . The chart reflects the person . . . the person reflects the chart . . . the chart reflects the Universe . . . the person reflects the Universe . . . They are all the same . . .

The purpose of interpretation is to find your own path . . . whatever that may mean to you . . . Every person's path is different — everyone has a unique birth chart.

Each sign is a face of God . . . each of us is evolving in our own unique, individual way. Astrology, clearly used, can reflect that evolution.

The Origin of Astrology

First, imagine this . . .

You are living about 10,000, or 50,000, years ago, on some beautiful part of this planet Earth . . .

Maybe you tend sheep, or maybe you are simply into star-gazing during the quiet nights . . . You spend many, many evenings looking into the clear night sky, and from the apparent chaos of all the stars, an order, a pattern emerges: you become aware of the constellations, the different, fixed patterns of all the stars . . . You find names for the patterns, describing their shapes and meanings, names like Orion the Hunter, the Scorpion, and the Great Bear, or the Big Dipper . . .

Then, you begin to notice the "Wanderers," or the "Planets" — the especially bright stars which do not belong in any constellation, but wander thru the night sky . . .

Then, you notice that the Wanderers, too, follow a pattern, a path in which they rise in the east and set in the west, like the Sun during the day. Each night, the Wanderers are seen against the backdrop of a certain constellation, but, over the weeks and months, they slowly and regularly move into other constellations . . . Because they all rise and set in about the same place, the "Wanderers" — including the Moon, and even the Sun — wander thru the same string of constellations, in a regular order. There happens to be 12 constellations in the string, making a full circle above and below the earth — this is the Zodiac — it is the backdrop against which we see the planets, always. The names of these constellations are familiar to you: Aries, Taurus, Gemini, and so on thru Pisces — then you come to Aries again . . .

Soon you become aware that the planets, moving thru the constellations, are a giant, cosmic clock with which you can measure time.

The Sun takes one year to travel thru all 12 signs of the Zodiac. The Moon takes only one month — the fastest moving "Planet" of all — which is why it is a symbol for change... (When, in astrology, you refer to the "Planets," you are also including the Sun and the Moon.)

Jupiter takes 12 years for a complete revolution thru the Zodiac ... and Saturn takes 28 or 29 years — a symbol for age, time, experience ... an important symbol for stages of evolution...

You can clearly see with the 'naked' eye the seven planets which were known to all ancient peoples: Sun, Moon, Mercury, Venus, Mars, Jupiter and Saturn.

Then, once you are aware of the regular, clocklike nature of the planetary cycles, you begin making the connections which truly gave birth to the ancient intuitive science and artform of astrology: You begin to notice correspondences with things that happen when certain planets are in certain signs. This phenomenon bears out the deep truth attributed to Hermes Trismegistus, who is said to have introduced advanced forms of astrology to the West at the beginning of the Egyptian era:

> *As above, so below;*
> *As below, so above.*

These connections were probably first made with the sun: when it enters into the sign (or constellation) of Aries, the first burst of Spring is here ... when the sun moves into Taurus, we settle into the middle of Spring ... when it moves into Gemini, changes start happening again ... unpredictable weather... When it moves into Cancer, Summer is here to stay... With Leo, we find the intense heat of mid-summer... With Virgo, we find things changing again... With Libra, Autumn bursts forth in all her beauty... When the sun goes into Scorpio, it gets stormy and tempestuous ... With Sagittarius comes the good cheer of the holiday season ... With Capricorn comes Winter and the mastery it requires ... With the month of Aquarius, we move into higher levels of being, making evolutionary leaps ... With the month of Pisces, we can experience the depth and death of Winter ... the deepest mystical awareness, beyond words...

So, by watching the Sun move thru the constellations, you could see (and therefore project and plan for) the year thru the seasons...

Within the general, monthly changes of the Sun cycle, then, you begin to notice the subtler, more rapidly changing influences of the Moon cycle — moving thru all 12 signs of the Zodiac every month.

By watching the Moon, and the other planets, and by noticing the changes which happen within you and around you as the Moon and the planets change signs, you begin to make a vast, subconscious (perhaps) catalog of the correspondences...

And astrology is born.

The Symbols of the Signs

Many of the keys to learning astrology are found within the symbols themselves . . . It's like learning the Tarot cards — the pictures themselves are the teachers, and can convey more information than thousands of words.

Look at the symbols for each sign, and sit with it . . . It may seem enigmatic — but just let each symbol soak into your deeper levels of being . . . There, it has a lot of meaning for you.

♈ **Aries, the Ram** . . . the symbol is a Ram's head — a symbol of energy bursting forth . . .

♉ **Taurus, the Bull** . . . the symbol is the Bull's head — a symbol of power, energy grounded in the Earth.

♊ **Gemini, the Twins** . . . the symbol is the Roman numeral II — a symbol of the nature of duality, the mind's ability to see and comprehend duality . . .

♋ **Cancer, the Crab, and the Cat** . . . the symbol represents the claws of the Crab, or a symbol of a woman's breasts, which it rules . . . A symbol of secret things, a symbol of the feminine nurturing principle.

♌ **Leo, the Lion** . . . the symbol is supposed to be the head and mane of a lion, a symbol of dynamic, powerful energy . . .

♍ **Virgo, the Virgin** . . . the symbol may represent matter coming back on itself, informing itself with energy — the M for matter, with the tail coming back upon itself — a symbol for accomplishment.

♎ **Libra, the Scales** ... the symbol is the Scales of Justice, a symbol of balance and harmony and awareness of all points of view.

♏ **Scorpio, the Scorpion, the Snake, and the Eagle** ... the symbol may represent matter soaring into the mystic — the M for matter, the tail bursting forth into creativity...

♐ **Sagittarius, the Archer** ... the symbol is the arrow, a symbol of physical travel, and intellectual and spiritual flight...

♑ **Capricorn, the Goat (or Sea-Goat)** ... the symbol is supposed to represent the head of a mountain goat, in some way — a symbol of leaping capability on the Earth...

♒ **Aquarius, the Water Bearer** ... the symbol represents the water of life, a symbol of spiritual nourishment from divine sources.

♓ **Pisces, the Fish** ... the symbol shows the heads of two fish, looking at each other — a symbol of flowing depths and oceanic consciousness...

Every sign has its power

Every sign has its own power, its own strength!

Aries has the strength of a ram, power to move forward, power to create the new, the life-giving power of Mars, the pro-creator . . .

Taurus has the strength of a bull, power to sustain life, the power of the earth. Buddha was a Taurus (often pictured touching the earth at his moment of Enlightenment).

Gemini has the strength of twins! The power of the mind — the ability to use the mind to create, to analyze, to communicate. The power of Mercury, the Messenger of the gods.

Cancer has the strength of a crab — tenacious, persistant, quick — and of a cat (another, higher symbol for Cancer) — aware, sensuous, magical, enlightened. The power of the Moon, the wellspring of intuition.

Leo has the strength of a Lion! Powerful, commanding, beautiful. The power of the Sun, the source of our life energy.

Virgo has the strength of a virgin — think of it! — the strength of a very young woman, with a vibrant, strong body, able to serve, able to heal, beautiful and promising. The power of Mercury, the Communicator of the gods (and, I feel, Virgo has the power of a distant and as yet undiscovered and unnamed planet which may become a symbol for enlightened service in the world).

Libra has the strength of the scales of justice — able to balance, to see all sides, to weigh all points of view. The power of Venus, the loved one — beautiful, commanding, magnetic.

Scorpio has the strength of a scorpion . . . and of a snake . . . and of an eagle. The scorpion: fierce, feared, stinging; the snake: healing energy flowing thru the body; the eagle: the far-seeing visionary, powerful, gifted. The power of Mars — strength and

22

fire — connected with the power of Pluto — the ultimate, the beyond.

Sagittarius has the strength of a centaur archer! Far-ranging, beautiful, outgoing, powerful. The power of Jupiter — eternal expansion and abundance.

Capricorn has the strength of a mountain goat — the power to climb mountains! Sure-footed, strong, tenacious, confident. The power of Saturn, the planet of wisdom which grows with age. Many masters have been Capricorns — including Joan of Arc.

Aquarius has the strength of an angel! Power to nourish, to uplift, to envision: to bring the Divine to Earth . . . The power of Uranus — the Awakener, which shows us that we are One with All.

Pisces has the strength of a Mystic . . . a fish* . . . the power of Pluto, the ultimate, the beyond, able to explore the depths of our minds, of our beings. I feel that Christ was a Pisces.

---

* Fish have always been symbols for the mystical qualities of the depths of the oceans. A fish was the early symbol of Christianity.

Lest I Appear Too Positive....

Sometimes people react to focusing on the strengths of each sign with a feeling that it is too positive, that we should include the weaknesses of each sign, too.

My response to this is to agree that each sign has its own characteristic weaknesses, but to stress that we should in no way let these weaknesses hinder us from tuning into our strengths. Don't give your own or anybody else's weaknesses too much power. Focus on your strengths and you are strong. Focus on your weaknesses and you are weak.

Yet it can be valuable to look at characteristic qualities of each sign which can use some improvement. There is a time when we must honestly look at our shortcomings, and focus on them long enough to realize that they are there, clearly see that they are not serving us, and clearly choose to let them go.

Aries energy can be insensitive, abrasive, egocentric, with a very short attention span. It needs the balance of Libra to make it aware of other people's feelings.

Taurus energy can be stubborn, resistant to change, and too preoccupied with the physical plane.

Gemini energy can be frenetically speedy, scattered, attempting to do too much at one time . . . Gemini's rational mind can forget the heart, the intuition, and get caught up in endless mental activity.

Cancer energy can be withdrawn, forgetting others, engulfed in emotion without dealing with it skillfully, filled with excuses.

Leo energy can be egocentric and shallow, always wanting to be the center of attention, unwilling to give others space and support.

Virgo energy can be critical, picky, constantly focusing on what is wrong with everything, including themselves.

Libra energy can be vain, self-centered, over-concerned with physical beauty, and constantly vascillating from one point of view or choice to the other. You'll often hear a Libra say, "On the other hand . . ."

Scorpio energy can be alternately stinging and withdrawn, hurting those they love, getting very intensely into emotional reactions.

Sagittarius can be careless, overly intellectual and talkative, superficially over-positive, and into far too many projects simultaneously.

Capricorn energy can be cold, remote, and secretly harshly judgemental of others, putting their career before their relationships and human warmth.

Aquarian energy can become unrealistic, spaced-out and dreamy, willing to visualize a million possibilities, but unwilling to focus on any of them long enough to accomplish anything.

Pisces energy can also become spaced-out, not relating to people, aloof, distant, sometimes heavily emotional and even self-destructive . . .

Again, I must stress that these weaknesses shouldn't be taken too seriously or given too much power, in relation to yourself or other people. We are all vast, complex beings, with many different qualities — strengths and weaknesses. Focus on your weaknesses long enough to clearly see them, shine the light of your understanding on them, and let them go. Then focus on your strengths, and fulfill your vision.

Prove it....

I don't attempt to prove anything about the validity of astrology. Most of the attempts to prove its validity seem to me to be as ridiculous as the attempts by so-called 'scientists' or anyone else to disprove its validity.

I simply see that it exists, and has existed for thousands of years, and that it has cataloged a large number of different correspondences which many people of many different cultures have apparently found meaningful and even useful. I see that some of these correspondences simply relate to the seasons of the year — the month of Aries is the advent of spring, the month of Leo is the height of summer... But many of the other correspondences seem to relate to other cycles which are subtler, perhaps reflecting more archtypal levels of our experience.

There's no need to prove it, or disprove it. It is a tool, a tool to use as you wish.

> "No one should hold it to be incredible that out of the astrologer's foolishness and blasphemies some useful and sacred knowledge may come."
>
> —Johaness Kepler

A Key to the Planets

Maybe you'll want to do this exercise with the planets that I recommend to people:

Just think of each of the names of the planets, relax, and picture it — fantasize, free associate, meditate with it, sit with it for a little while . . . Whatever happens is all right . . . (The Sun and the Moon, too, are included among the 'planets'.)

Think of them as totally as you can — mythologically and/or scientifically and/or cosmically and/or whatever comes to mind . . .

> *Mercury . . . Venus . . . Mars . . . Jupiter . . .*
> *Saturn . . . Uranus . . . Neptune . . . Pluto . . .*
> *Sun . . . Moon . . .*

Most of these words have a lot of associations for us . . . and these associations are a key to understanding the power of these planets.

Within our mythological heritage — deep wellsprings of intuitive information — each of these planetary forces has been envisioned in human form, as energies we can comprehend, feel, and summon . . .

A Key to the Signs

*The 12 signs are the 12 faces of God — the 12 states of
perfect being — each with their unevolved, evolving,
and evolved levels of being.*

Instead of 'faces of God' you may want to use the words 'states
of perfect being' or 'states of higher consciousness' or 'levels of
divine being' or whatever... The specific words aren't important — choose whatever words resonate most deeply for you.

Astrology is a ritual / a game / an intuitive science / a form of
prayer / a connection with higher intelligence which involves
identifying with symbols. These symbols gain deep meaning —
intuitive meaning — when and only when we look deeply into
the symbols, when we observe their inner (or *esoteric*) meanings
and resonances.

If we're going to identify with a symbol, like a Sun Sign, it might
as well be a high one ... a deep one ... a powerful one — a face
of God.

Many of the current popular conceptions of astrology are still
suffering from Victorian and even Puritan hangovers. Most of
the understanding of the signs relates only to the lower, unevolved side of the symbols ... and the evolution of the symbol, the power of the symbol, is lost, forgotten.

*Each sign is a sign of transformation... The un-
evolved is the 'ground', or starting point... The
evolving is the 'path', or direction of growth...
The evolved is the 'goal', or the fruit of the search.*

28

Unevolved, Evolving, and Evolved....

This is one of the most beautiful discoveries of New Age astrology: each and every sign has its unevolved, evolving, and evolved characteristics. Each and every sign is a path to perfection. Each sign has its own unique power and insight.

The symbols associated with Scorpio contain this key very clearly. Scorpio is the sign of transfiguration, transformation:

Unevolved Scorpio energy is symbolized by the Scorpion — stinging, poisonous.

Evolving Scorpio energy is symbolized by the Snake, winding up the cadeusus of the spine — a powerful healing force ... energy rising up the energy centers of the spine...

Evolved Scorpio has undergone a complete, magical transformation, into the Eagle (or the Phoenix). The Eagle's vision, it is said, is so keen that it can spot a mouse from half a mile in the air ... and it flies closer to the Sun than any other creature...

The Eagle is a symbol of spiritual flight ... complete freedom...

The Phoenix destroys itself to be reborn anew from its old ashes — a symbol of Autumn, the time of Scorpio, of death ... and beyond death thru transformation into new life...

Focus on the *evolving* qualities of each sign, and you are given deep tools of growth. The basic key at this level is this:

> *The evolving qualities use the same energies as the unevolved qualities of each sign – but they are used in conscious, creative, useful ways which lead to growth, to health, and to the dissolving of limitations.*

Focus upon the *evolved* aspects of each sign, and you unlock deep intuitive resources of knowledge.

A Deep, Ancient Truth

There is a deep, ancient truth which surfaces here:

> *The very 'negative' emotions themselves provide the energy which causes transformation into a higher state of being . . .*

The unevolved qualities of each sign are the same thing as the evolved qualities — it is all energy . . . the only difference is the level of vibration.

Our very weaknesses give us the strength for growth.

In the brilliant teachings of Tibetan Buddhism, this key (to inner growth, to light, to whatever you wish) is expressed very clearly: They teach that there are basically five different general categories of 'negative' — or separating, alienating, contracting — emotions. (In Tibetan, the word for these emotions is the same word as 'poisons' — for they can indeed poison us, so that we do not experience the true purity of our being.)

Each of these 'negative' emotions, when confronted, clearly looked at, and by doing so, understood, becomes changed, transmuted into one of the five wisdoms:

When we look at our ignorance, we can truly find deep understanding — the wisdom which comprehends the ultimate nature of reality.

When we look at our pride or arrogance, we can find the wisdom of equanimity — the vision which sees the oneness of everything.

When we confront our jealousy and careless passion, we can discover the "discriminating wisdom" — the power to differentiate and analyze. In some respects, this is the opposite of the wisdom which sees the oneness of everything.

When we openly confront our fears, we can find the "all-accomplishing wisdom" — the ability to take care of business.

When we confront our anger, it becomes transmuted into the "mirror-like wisdom" — the ability to be a mirror for others, to reflect their true nature and level of awareness.

A message to myself —

> *Don't reject the sadness,*
> *Don't reject the sorrow,*
> *Don't reject the suffering*
> *And the pain*

> *Blessed are these things*
> *For thru them we grow*
> *Into true understanding*
> *Of our way*

What is a Chart?

A chart is a picture which represents the solar system — quite accurately, actually — as it appeared or will appear to us at any particular time in which we are interested.

The Ascendant, or the line directly off to the left from the center (at the 9 o'clock position), represents the Eastern horizon, where the Sun and the Moon and all the planets rise. The Midheaven (at the 12 o'clock position) shows which planets are directly overhead. The cusp between the 6th and 7th houses (at the 3 o'clock position) is the Western horizon, and the Nadir (opposite the Midheaven, at the 6 o'clock position) shows what planets were directly below us, below the horizon.

Because the solar system is relatively flat (with the exception of Pluto, which is way off the plane of the rest of the solar system), it appears to us here on Earth as if the Sun and Moon and all the planets rise in the same place, travel thru a similar path thru the skies — the 'ecliptic' — and set in the same place. The background of this path just happens to be a series of 12 constellations, which from ancient times have been known to us as the Zodiac, and which form a convenient means of mapping the positions of the planets. For purposes of convenience, each constellation is said to comprise exactly 30° of the circle (so that the 12 constellations equal 360°, the full circle).

So, a chart is an actual map of the solar system, as it appears from earth. If you were born at noon, the Sun will be directly overhead, in the Midheaven; if you were born at sunset, it will be on the 6th-7th house cusp, the 'Descendant'; if you were born at dawn, it will be on the Ascendant; if you were born at midnight, it will be on the Nadir.

All of these are considered power points.

Your chart is a picture....

Your birth chart is a picture of the constellations and planets around you at birth...

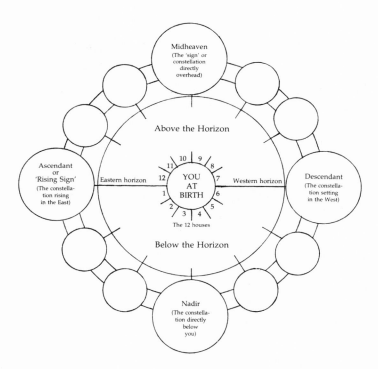

Midheaven
(The 'sign' or constellation directly overhead)

Above the Horizon

Ascendant or 'Rising Sign' (The constellation rising in the East)

Eastern horizon

Descendant (The constellation setting in the West)

Western horizon

YOU AT BIRTH

The 12 houses

Below the Horizon

Nadir (The constellation directly below you)

An astrological chart is a mandala, a picture of yourself... Just gazing at it in its general form can give you a lot of information...

The 12 Houses start with the first House at the Ascendant, and move counter-clockwise, dividing the whole cycle of existence into 12 different phases or areas of experience. The Houses are numbered 1-12 on the chart blank.

The Hemispheres

There are two different sets of hemispheres in a chart — dividing it East and West, and North and South.

By dividing the chart East and West (left and right, like the top diagram, opposite page), we have the path of Will on the left, and the path of Surrender on the right...

People with planets predominantly on the left side of their chart will deal primarily with *will* — the conscious directing of their course. People with planets predominantly on the right side of their chart will deal primarily with *surrender* — acceptance, going with the flow, like water...

By dividing the chart North and South (like the bottom diagram, opposite page) we have two other hemispheres, the path of the Sun above, and the path of the Moon below.

People with planets predominantly on the top half of their chart will deal with activity in the world (and beyond, if it gets into the 11th and 12th houses). People with planets predominantly on the bottom half of their chart will deal primarily with inner growth and inner being.

The Hemispheres

The Path of Fire
Will
Directing your course

The Path of Water
Surrender
Tao
Going with the flow . . .

The Path of the Sun
Activity
in the World
(& beyond)

Inner growth
&
Being
The Path of the Moon

Key Words

Each sign, planet and house is a very rich symbol.

I sometimes call the following pages of *key words* my 'instant intuitive astrology system':

Take a keyword from one symbol and link it together with any other keyword from another symbol, for any combination you're interested in. You have then formed a compound keyword symbol.

Then just sit with it, absorb it intuitively. Perhaps it won't make any sense to you at all — then just toss it away and try again with some different keywords from the same categories.

For example, if your Sun is in Virgo, and you're wondering what that means, choose a keyword for 'Sun' — say 'life force' — and link it with a key word for 'Virgo' — say 'Earth, changing':

'Life force, Earth, changing'
or
'The individual, capable'

Just absorb these words ... let your imagination go ... free associate ...

Note how the houses are similar in meaning to their corresponding signs ... they follow a similar progression — the first house is the natural house of Aries, the second house is the natural house of Taurus, and so on.

After the planets, signs, and houses, I've also included the 'special points' and the 'aspects' — the only other factors I use in a complete interpretation.

Key Words - Planets

Planets (symbols of different types and levels of energy):

☉ Sun: life force; the individual; personality; central, basic
energy; the self; creativity.

☾ Moon: intuition; emotions; the secret being; psychic energy;
'collective unconscious'; the inner being, beyond
personality; unity with all.

☿ Mercury: mental energy; the active mind; the rational mind;
communication ability; the messenger of the gods;
thought.

♀ Venus: love energy; beauty; happiness; harmony; balance;
romance; women; yin energy; heart chakra;
feminine aspect.

♂ Mars: basic physical energy; power center; yang energy;
men; 3rd chakra; strength; male aspect; the seed of
creation.

♃ Jupiter: expansive energy; positive, beneficial energy;
ever-growing; laws of attraction; the Ruler.

♄ Saturn: wisdom that grows with age; 'constrictive' energy;
limiting; simplifying; focusing; mature; old age;
experience; mastery.

♅ Uranus: 7th chakra ('crown') energy; explosive; crazy
wisdom; change; transcendental energy; the
innovator; cosmic consciousness; Awakener.

♆ Neptune: 6th chakra ('3rd eye') energy; calm and clear
wisdom; interpenetration; visionary; psychic; the
magician.

♇ Pluto: the beyond; beyond words; beyond all models;
explosive change; dance of Shiva; transcendental.

Key Words - Signs

Signs (symbols of different types and expressions of energy)

♈ **Aries:** Fiery, creative; the Ram; ruled by Mars energy; ego; bursting forth; the child; Spring; the creative force of spirit.
Unevolved: egocentric, overly aggressive, insensitive.
Evolved: the Initiator, the Creator.

♉ **Taurus:** Earth, sustaining; the Bull; ruled by Venus energy; connected to the Earth; solidity; grounded; the wisdom of the Earth; the Buddha.
Unevolved: grasping, materialistic, stubborn.
Evolved: the Master at One with the Earth.

♊ **Gemini:** Air, changing; the Twins; ruled by Mercury energy; the communicator; channel; the duality of existence.
Unevolved: rampant rational mind, split personality.
Evolved: the channel of divine intelligence.

♋ **Cancer:** Water, creative; the Crab; the Cat; ruled by the Moon; quiet, looking inward; the Mother; the MoonChild; psychic.
Unevolved: the Crab, withdrawn, avoiding.
Evolved: the Cat, the Master of sub- and super-conscious forces; the Magician; the Witch (ie, 'Wise One').

♌ **Leo:** Fiery, sustaining; the Lion; ruled by the Sun; the performer; the creative artist; dynamic; shining forth.
Unevolved: egocentric, needing attention.
Evolved: the Sun King, shining light on all.

♍ **Virgo:** Earth, changing; the Virgin; ruled by Mercury energy; delicate; capable; selfless servant; healer; analytical.
Unevolved: critical of self and others, overwhelmed by details.
Evolved: the Master of Discriminating Wisdom, a healer.

♎ Libra: Air, creative; the Scales; ruled by Venus; beautiful; balanced; artistic; harmonizing; justice with compassion; in relationship.
Unevolved: judgmental, undecided, vain.
Evolved: the Master of Love.

♏ Scorpio: Water, sustaining; the Scorpion; the Snake; the Eagle or Phoenix; ruled by Mars on one octave, Pluto on another; dynamic; 'fire of water'; transformation; rules sexual organs.
Unevolved: stinging, harmful, intense emotions.
Evolved: the Master of Tantra, of life's forces.

♐ Sagittarius: Fiery, changing; the Archer; ruled by Jupiter; expansive; the philosopher; the traveller; friendly; jovial; Santa Claus; the Renaissance ideal.
Unevolved: scattered, excessive.
Evolved: the Master of Infinite possibilities!

♑ Capricorn: Earth, creative; the Sea-Goat; ruled by Saturn; capable; focused; the master of the earthly plane; Pan.
Unevolved: constricted, excessively serious, miserly.
Evolved: the Master, effortlessly accomplishing on the material plane.

♒ Aquarius: Air, sustaining; the Water-Bearer; the Angel; ruled by Uranus; the Forerunner; the futurist; spacy; the herald of the new age of universal brotherhood and sisterhood; children of the new dawn; the inventor.
Unevolved: negative, empty, scattered, excessive.
Evolved: the Master Magician; the Pathfinder.

♓ Pisces: Water, changing; the Fish; ruled by Neptune on one octave, Pluto on another; the visionary; the psychic; the destroyer (Shiva); the end of the cycle; the ultimate; shimmering emptiness (*Shunyata*).
Unevolved: spaced-out, dark, empty, wasteful, self-destructive.
Evolved: the Master, the Christ.

Key Words - Houses

Houses (symbols of areas of experience)

1st: the Rising Sign; outer personality; physical appearance; what others see; the individual; the ego; the place of the spontaneous, here-and-now wisdom of a child.

2nd: personal resources; strengths; possessions; physical plane surroundings; money.

3rd: communication; mental activity; how you speak to the world; short-distance travel; brothers and sisters.

4th: ground, center; home, mother; environment you live in; deepest strength within; inner refuge.

5th: self-expression; entertainment; performing; creative expression; children.

6th: service to others; health; healing; loving and serving.

7th: relations to other individuals; marriage; partnerships; contracts; relationships.

8th: deep relationships; sexual relations; birth and death and transformation; tantra; finding the keys to ultimate understanding within daily life, rejecting nothing.

9th: growth; education; education into new areas; philosophy; religion; infinite possibilities; the Renaissance ideal; long-distance travel; publishing.

10th: work in the world; career; material plane mastery; achievement; recognition.

11th: beyond the material plane; ideals; mental and spiritual planes; goals; innovations; compassion; visions; dreams; the Bodhisattva path.

12th: the end of the cycle; transformation; destruction and beyond; ultimate reality; psychic awareness; what you already know from past lives.

Key Words-Special Points

Special Points in a Chart

☊ North Node of the Moon: the 'Dragon's head': your place of strength and protection. You always have a source of power here.

☋ South Node of the Moon: the 'Dragon's tail': your 'place of self-undoing' — where you can learn your deepest lessons, where you can go beyond ego, beyond limiting concepts of self.

⊗ Fortune: where you will find your true fortune this lifetime.

Aspects

☌ Conjunction (planets within 4° of each other): energies are combined; flowing together; united.

△ Trine (planets 120° apart, ± 4°): powerfully flowing together; united.

✳ Sextile (planets 60° apart, ± 4°): flowing together positively.

□ Square (planets 90° apart, ± 4°): may be some kind of blockage; an opportunity for growth; a blessing to teach us something.

☍ Opposition (planets 180° apart, ± 4°): may be apparent opposition; always perfect balance on a deeper level; opposite and complementary.

Meditations on Your Chart

This is the art of interpretation in a nutshell.

Look at your birth ('natal') chart. Or look at anyone's chart. See that it is a gift. Within it are many strengths, many blessings. Within it is a key to understanding yourself.

Within it is a starting point, a path, and a goal.

Every sign is a face of God.

☉ See where the Sun is — what sign, what house — you will express yourself, your own unique life force and individuality, generally, thru these particular qualities and energies.

☾ See where the Moon is — your intuitive awareness is open here . . . this is a key beyond yourself. Within the particular energies of your moon sign you can find deep, intuitive understanding.

☿ See where Mercury is — rational mind has strengths and abilities here . . . you can communicate well thru this sign, and this house . . . on an esoteric level, this is your place of communication with God — with divine forces.

♀ See where Venus is — your love is here, your sense of beauty is here, your heart can open here . . . on an esoteric level, this is where you can understand the true nature of the Universe, the force of creation, preservation, and destruction: Love . . .

♂ See where Mars is — you have physical strengths here, this is your point of power . . . you can open 2nd (sensitivity, sensation) and 3rd (power) chakras here, find powerful creative energies ... you may have ego conflicts here.

♃ See where Jupiter is — you have strong, expansive, positive energy here ... good fortune, growth...

♄ See where Saturn is — the wisdom that grows with age is here ... you will receive teachings here, you will deepen and grow in life's experiences here ... focus and understanding are here.

♅ See where Uranus is — change is here, shattering previous models of behavior ... crazy wisdom ... Union with the All is here — Uranus is the planet of the 7th ('Crown') chakra, which can open up to unite with the whole Universe...

♆ See where Neptune is — calm and clear wisdom is here, psychic capabilities, awareness of the 'sub-' and 'super-' consciousness — Neptune is the planet of the '3rd eye', the 6th chakra, between your brows, the place of inner vision, dreams, higher realms.

♇ See where Pluto is — the beyond is here...

☊ See where the North Node of the Moon is — you have protection and strength here.

☋ See where the South Node of the Moon is — you have an opportunity to go beyond self here, to go beyond limited conceptions of who you think you are, a place of 'self-undoing' in some form, a place of growth, letting go.

⊗ See where Fortune is — you have your true fortune here.

See what the Rising Sign is — this is how others see you.

See what the Midheaven is — this is your activity in the world.

See what the Nadir is — this is your true, deep inner source, your home, your center, your ground.

See where your conjunctions, trines, and sextiles are — this is flowing, connected energy, blending smoothly together.

See where your squared aspects are — these are your challenges, possibly 'obstacles', teachings, the places where you grow.

See where your oppositions are — these may seem opposing, contradictory forces . . . but within them are always found perfect balance, perfect necessary harmony. By understanding these so-called 'oppositions', you can understand a great deal about yourself.

Outer, Inner and Secret....

Your chart is a guide to your outer, inner, and secret levels of being...

Your Rising Sign is the outer — showing how others see you, how you relate to the world...

Your Sun Sign is the inner — showing your personality, and how you feel about yourself... It shows your heart's choice, your path...

Your Moon Sign is the 'secret' level of being, the deepest, reaching to the ultimate ... the key to your connection with the Macrocosm...

Everyone, everything, every act, every event has its outer, inner and secret levels of being...

The Sun thru the Year

The Sun's yearly journey thru all the signs reflects each sign as it reflects the changes that the year naturally flows thru . . . Every month brings a different energy, first *yang* (outgoing, relating to others), then *yin* (inward going, deepening):

Spring bursts forth	First, the rush of spring . . . high, creative, outgoing energy.	—Aries ♈
Spring is here to stay	Then, a deeper, slower rhythm, a time for grounding, growing roots, connecting with the sustaining energies of the Earth.	—Taurus ♉
Spring changes into	Then, another high energy time of changes . . . Spring changes . . . A time to move out and communicate.	—Gemini ♊
Summer!	Summer unfolds . . . energy settles down again . . . A time to be home, grounded, growing, flowing.	—Cancer ♋
Mid-Summer	The intense Sun brings people out into the light . . . a time to share, relate, perform.	—Leo ♌
Late Summer changes into	Summer withdraws . . . a time to love, serve, and remember . . . to heal and prepare . . .	—Virgo ♍
Autumn	The most beautiful, spectacular month . . . Fall in all its colors bursts forth . . . A time of inspiration, a time to relate to others.	—Libra ♎

Mid-Autumn	Now, a time of transformation — changes . . . the death of the year. Turbulence without, insight within. Daily life provides many insights.	—Scorpio ♏
Late Autumn	A strong, boisterous, outgoing energy . . . abundance everywhere! The spirit of Thanksgiving and Christmas . . . confident, positive.	—Sagittarius ♐
Early Winter	A month of accomplishment . . . A time to take care of business, to grow, to focus, to deepen . . . Saturn energy is in the air: the wisdom that grows with age.	—Capricorn ♑
Mid-Winter	A month of spontaneous exhuberance . . . new ideas . . . surprises . . . light amidst the darkness of winter . . . Crazy wisdom emerges.	—Aquarius ♒
Late Winter	The end of Winter . . . the end of the cycle . . . the deep, mysterious, mystical transfiguration of the year . . . Meditation provides many insights, keys to ultimate understanding . . . Relax, and go within during this month.	—Pisces ♓

Watching the Moon

Get a calendar which shows you what sign the Moon is in. Meditate with, flow with, let yourself feel each of the signs as the Moon goes thru them.

The Moon's energy affects us on deep, subtle intuitive and emotional levels ... and as it passes thru each sign, there's a definite vibrational feel to each, and a definite vibrational change as the Moon changes sign.

Watching the Sun tunes us into a yearly cycle, with major changes every month ... Watching the Moon tunes us into a monthly cycle, with emotional and intuitive changes every two days or so ... Here's a general guide:

♈
yang
When the Moon goes into **Aries**, act! Move! Mars energy! Kick out the jams! Begin projects. Watch your temper. The strength of the Ram is in the air.

♉
yin
When the Moon goes into **Taurus**, relax ... go with the flow, slow down ... With the energy of the Bull in the air, much can be accomplished, especially on an earthly, physical level, but the Bull moves at his own pace, and it's best not to try to speed him up ... Enjoy your body ... and your loved ones ...

♊
yang
When the Moon goes into **Gemini**, take care of business, buzz around, communicate! Mercury energy is rampant ... Good time for writing, travel, activity, working efficiently.

♋
yin
When the Moon goes into **Cancer**, slow down again ... recharge, relax ... good time to be home ... look within — intuitive channels are open...

When the Moon goes into **Leo**, let your light shine! Go out steppin' . . . or whatever you wish to do. Speak your truth for all to hear — this is a time to express yourself creatively, to perform. Sun energy is in the air!

yang

When the Moon is in **Virgo**, it's a much more delicate energy . . . a good time to take care of business, especially details . . . discriminating wisdom is very strong . . . but don't let it get into too much criticism of self or others . . . love, serve, remember — devotion to others can bring true happiness . . . Mercury energy is brought to Earth.

yin

When the Moon is in **Libra**, Venus energy is strong . . . a good time to relate to others . . . to be with a lover . . . to have harmonious group meetings and social events . . . to open your heart.

yang

When the Moon is in **Scorpio**, things might get heavy — they certainly will get deep . . . In this kind of energy is always a key to transformation . . . Don't reject your emotional nature . . . use it as a tool for growth . . .

yin

When the Moon is in **Sagittarius**, enjoy! Great time to party, and/or study and grow . . . The Renaissance ideal — interest and capability in a wide range of areas — flourishes . . . an outgoing, positive time.

yang

When the Moon is in **Capricorn**, take care of business! This can be a time of effortless accomplishment. Saturn energy is in the air — the wisdom that grows with age . . . See what needs to be done, and focus on a way of doing it.

yin

When the Moon is in **Aquarius**, let go! Enjoy! Tune in to the dawn of a new age, to great change everywhere! Connect with your divine nature! An exhuberant, sometimes even euphoric time . . . Crazy wisdom, Uranus energy is in the air, for all who are sensitive enough to feel it . . .

yang

When the Moon is in **Pisces**, let go! Let it be . . . A mystic is within you — reflect and deepen.

yin

49

The Moon Cycle

Watch . . .

Just before the New Moon (when the Moon is conjunct with the Sun), there may be a time of questioning . . . the three days before the New Moon may be dark or difficult in some way — deep teachings are here . . . It is the time known as the "dark of the moon."

At the New Moon, there is a flooding of light and awareness . . . New Moon is a time to begin things . . .

The first week after the New Moon, energy builds . . . It is a time to focus on what you've begun, and develop it . . .

The second week after the New Moon, which concludes with the Full Moon (when the Moon is opposite the Sun), is filled with energy and momentum . . . the best time to express, accomplish, to teach.

The third week (the week after the Full Moon) is the time of culmination: the best time to bring to fruition . . .

The fourth week is the time of concluding and renewal . . . a time to relax and go within . . . to reflect . . . Don't start projects in the fourth quarter . . .

As the Moon gets more and more full, psychic and emotional energies increase . . . The New Moon and the Full Moon are both especially powerful and propitious times . . .

The Sun & Moon thru the Signs

Here's a direct path to the conscious use of the tool of astrology
... tuning into the strengths, the power, of each sign...

The Sun stays in each sign for a month ... the Moon moves
thru each sign in two days or so (28 days for a whole cycle thru
the 12 signs — a "lunar month")...

When the Sun or Moon is in **Aries**, celebrate your connection
with all life ... burst forth like the little green plants thru the
snow, like a child, spontaneous and creative and free...

When the Sun or Moon is in **Taurus**, celebrate your connection
with the Earth... Tune into your body, or a lover's body, or
anybody, and heal and love and bless... A Taurus chant:

> *O Earthly Mother, thank you for this beautiful day*
> *May we open up our hearts*
> *that we may be with you*
> *all the way, all the way*

Buddha was a Taurus, touching the Earth at his moment of
Enlightenment, and looking up at the Morning Star: Venus.

When the Sun or Moon is in **Gemini**, celebrate your mind! What
an instrument it is! What capabilities! Your mind has within it all
of the power of Mercury, the winged Messenger of the Gods —
that is, communication from divine sources within... The
mind is a tool for instant, magical creation, with the speed of
thought...

When the Sun or Moon is in **Cancer, the MoonChild**, celebrate
your inner depths... Enjoy being alone ... looking within...
Enjoy your infinite depth ... your infinite inner vision ...
your infinite emptiness and bliss...

> *Look within, and you find*
> *Every answer you need*

51

The kingdom of heaven
is within

When the Sun or Moon is in **Leo**, the Sun Lion, celebrate yourself! Let your light shine — like the Sun, on *all* others . . . Get out . . . party . . . enjoy . . . be a performer . . . Speak your truth for all to hear . . . Learn to act without needing anyone else's approval . . . Just do your thing . . . and enjoy! Life is a game to be played — not a problem to be solved . . .

When the Sun or Moon is in **Virgo**, celebrate your capabilities . . . Virgo is the power of Mercury brought to Earth . . . and so Virgo energy can heal, serve, do things that really aid and assist on a physical level the manifestation of the transformations which are taking place on physical, emotional, mental, and spiritual levels . . . Virgo is the power of discriminating wisdom . . . the use of rational mind to see what things can change and finding the strength and insight to change them.

When the Sun or Moon is in **Libra**, celebrate the beauty of all Creation . . . Celebrate love, symbolized by Venus . . . Open your heart to love, to others, to relationships . . . The greatest joy in life is loving — others, yourself, even *things* . . .

"A new law I give to you:
Love one another . . ."

There is an artist within you . . . a lover . . . an exquisite beauty . . . ever being re-born . . . thru love . . .

When the Sun or Moon is in **Scorpio**, celebrate every moment, everything — even the darkest parts of yourself . . . Celebrate the path of *tantra*: seeing the perfection within every moment, rejecting nothing . . . Celebrate the eternal transformation which the force of life is ever going thru . . . The Scorpion becomes the Snake, winding up the cadeusus of the spine, which becomes the Eagle or the Phoenix, symbols of spiritual flight and transformation . . .

When the Sun or Moon is in **Sagittarius**, celebrate the infinite possibilities within your reach! Celebrate your many accomplishments, your many lives and roles and abilities ... and celebrate and explore the many possibilities ahead... Grow, ever greater... Expand... Evolution is an endless process — you will continue to grow, until you are a being of pure light! Be like the Renaissance ideal in this new Renaissance: capable in so many different areas, an eternal student, an eternal teacher...

When the Sun or Moon is in **Capricorn**, express your capabilities! Capricorn is the sign of Creative Earth: creative capability on the material plane to manifest whatever your heart desires... Capricorn is the sign of the Master... As Joel Goldsmith said: "Act like a master, and the power will be given to you to *be* a master." You have the power within you to effortlessly accomplish whatever you wish ... simply focus on it, be patient, and persistant, and it will unfold, in its own time... There is no barrier at all, for the person aware of the Infinity of Time and Space ... which leads to...

When the Sun or Moon is in **Aquarius**, celebrate the dawning of the New Age... Celebrate total freedom ... an age in which all social models are shattered ... an age in which you are free to do as you dream... Explore your dreams ... your visions ... your ideals ... your highest aspirations... You have the power to achieve them... Aquarius is ruled by Uranus, a symbol of the energy of the 7th Chakra, the Crown, which unites with the Cosmos... Cosmic Consciousness is here and now...

When the Sun or Moon is in **Pisces**, celebrate the mystic within you ... the mystery of all being ... of all life... Celebrate the path of seeing the perfection which is beyond daily life, beyond all earthly activity, even beyond our dreams and imaginings and visions and ideals (symbols of Aquarius and the 11th house)... Celebrate Being... Celebrate Seeing... Pisces is ruled by both Neptune and Pluto, the two outermost planets... Neptune is a symbol of the energy of the 6th Chakra, the 3rd eye: inner vision ... the eye of understanding ... of interpenetration ... of visualization ... of magic creation... Pluto is beyond ... beyond words... Listen to the depths of your deepest stillness...

53

What Does the Moonsign Do?

Watching the Moon, and seeing which sign it's in, can tune us into our own natural physical/emotional cycles. Whether it's thru bio-rhythms, or emotional ups and downs, or energy levels, or observing the Moonsign, it's useful to have some sort of gauge or tool measuring our ever-changing cycles of emotions and energy.

If we observe our emotional states over a period of time, a pattern emerges. Bio-rhythms and Moonsign cycles map out these patterns.

Like all other tools, Moonsigns are sometimes used skillfully and sometimes unskillfully. Used skillfully, watching the Moonsign can tune us into the flowing changes that we're always going thru, the alternations between being active and passive, outer-directed and inner-turning, yin and yang . . .

> To everything, there is a season . . .

Used skillfully, we can tune into the strengths of each sign . . . (Used unskillfully, we tune into the *weaknesses* of each sign, and use the Moonsign or our own Sunsign as an excuse for not confronting something or not accomplishing something.)

Watch what sign the Moon is in — and watch how you feel . . . and how others feel . . . Every month, the Moon travels thru all 12 signs — the complete cycle. Watch it for several cycles, and you'll become aware of all kinds of correspondences . . . Keep watching it, and a pattern will emerge . . . a pattern which incorporates all our varied feelings and actions . . .

One thing watching the Moon teaches you is patience. And that all things pass.

Another thing it teaches is the art and science of astrology itself — your recurring pattern of feelings as the Moon passes thru each sign teaches more about that sign than reading a great number of words about other people's experiences and ideas and interpretations . . .

Conventional Astrology: Uses & Misuses

There's a lot of unskillful use of the tool of astrology in today's newspapers and books and interpretations. But that doesn't mean that the tool is not useful — it just means that it has been misused. Let's not judge something by the way it has been misused by some people...

I studied "conventional" astrology for several years, and then let it go ... gave it up ... because I was not at all satisfied with the results of conventional astrology... People used it so often as an excuse, a justification for their weaknesses and shortcomings, and a way of blaming other people for their least evolved characteristics.

But then, later, I met some Sufis who were into astrology in a whole new way. And I met a very fine teacher from Tibet, who was also into astrology in a whole new way ... a way that promoted growth, rather than inhibiting it in any way.

Now, as I look back on 'conventional' astrology, I see it in a whole new light: I see how it reflects the mentality of some very worn-out Victorian and even Puritan concepts and core beliefs...

For there are several things in popular or conventional astrology which are things to fear — like the planet Saturn, the 12th house, the signs of Scorpio and Pisces, and the South Node of the Moon... And there are many, many other things which are seen in a somewhat clouded, vague, unclear light, like the signs of Virgo and Capricorn, and the planet Neptune, and aspects which are square or in opposition... And all of these interpretations lead to chart readings which have many areas of avoidance and regret and limitation — all of which are unnecessary...

56

Now, a 'new' (actually, an ancient) astrology is emerging, which reflects a 'new', clearer way of living and looking at things.

Puritan and Victorian models of how it should be have long ago crumbled, undermined by the Existentialist awakening, and totally obliterated by the New Age awakening. And it is time that our astrological models and concepts change too...

The planet Saturn is no longer seen as a force of limitation and constriction — instead, it is seen as the wisdom which grows with age ... the power of growth and experience ... the power to focus energies...

The 12th house is no longer seen as the house of prisons and confinement and deep, dark fears that are hidden in the closets of the darkest recesses of our hidden subconscious minds — instead, it is seen as the final house, the culmination of all understanding ... ultimate truths lie there ... and it is also seen to contain that which we deeply, intuitively, effortlessly know from past lives or past experience...

Scorpio and Pisces are no longer feared or rejected — instead, they are seen as signs of transformation, beauty and wonder... Scorpio, very much a part of this world and all its widely varying energies, and Pisces very much beyond this world, with its high, fine, psychic energies ... its mystical vision.

Thru the Year

A good meditation for the month of . . .

. . . **Aries** is springing forth . . . new beginnings . . . the joy of a child . . .

. . . **Taurus** is relaxing . . . centering, grounding . . . relating to the Earth and Nature . . .

. . . **Gemini** is sharpening, skillfully using rational mind.

. . . **Cancer** is finding the 'baseline happiness' within . . . turning inward for answers.

. . . **Leo** is turning outward, letting your light shine . . .

. . . **Virgo** is loving and serving and healing.

. . . **Libra** is being beautiful, creating beauty and harmony around you.

. . . **Scorpio** is accepting the teachings of every moment, rejecting none . . . the transformation of every moment . . .

. . . **Sagittarius** is finding the infinite possibilities for our minds to explore and evolve and learn and grow!

. . . **Capricorn** is the effortless mastery on the physical plane, the 'all-accomplishing wisdom' . . .

. . . **Aquarius** is letting go! Being free here and now . . . free to be unique, changeable . . . whatever your heart desires.

. . . **Pisces** is discovering the deepest inner wonder of it all . . . the Ultimate . . . the mystical . . . the Silence.

Compatibility/Incompatibility

Conventional astrology teaches that certain signs are compatible with certain other signs and incompatible with other signs . . . (It is said that Air and Fire signs are compatible, Earth and Water signs are compatible, but Air-Earth, Air-Water, and Fire-Earth, Fire-Water combinations are incompatible.)

I feel that this view is limited and incorrect, for several reasons:

First of all, it is based on only a Sun sign generalization, and people have much more depth and complexity than merely their Sun signs.

But most importantly: it has not proven true in my experience. I am a Cancer, a MoonChild . . . My two longest-lasting and most meaningful love relationships have been with an Aries and a Libra — two signs I am supposedly incompatible with! My other main sustained romantic interest has been with a Sagittarius — another sign I am not supposed to be compatible with . . . And I have found these relationships to be *highly* compatible . . .

In fact, I find that relationships between the so-called 'incompatible' signs are often the most fruitful, because each partner has so much to teach the other: different ways of seeing, new and different ways of reacting. By enlarging our perspective, we grow.

So I feel that, in their essence, all signs are compatible — each is a perfect part of a perfect whole . . .

Transits

Looking at transits — where the planets are *now* — adds a whole new beautiful dimension to astrology . . . A great deal of meaning can surface, showing what's happening, and even getting into the very useful art of divination, showing what's going to happen . . .

In looking at where the planets are now, or will be in the future, or were in the past at any given time, you can get a great deal of information in a short time. All you need is an *Ephemeris* — a table of planetary positions. Look at where the planets are *now* — or any other time you're interested in. Just doing this can give you much information . . . Take your time, see what sign each planet is in, and sit with it awhile . . .

Then, place the transiting planets around your birth chart — or around the chart of anyone or anything you're interested in . . .

Notice the houses in which planetary activity is going on . . . Notice any conjunctions of transiting planets with your planets at birth — there's special significance here, a special uniting of the energies of those two planets . . . Notice any squares or oppositions — this may reflect a difficulty, a challenge and/or an area of growth . . .

Watch the planets . . . It's especially useful to watch the Sun and the Moon . . . Notice when they change signs, notice how you feel and act, and how others feel and act . . . This is a beautiful way to find a key to your own understanding on deep, intuitive levels.

The Saturn Cycle ♄

The Saturn Cycle is a very important part of astrological interpretation. It moves the interpretation into the realm of transits, which takes into account where the planets have travelled since the moment of the birth chart.

Each planet takes a certain amount of time to travel thru all 12 signs and return to its original position in any given chart. The Moon takes only a month. The Sun takes a year . . . Mercury and Venus stay close to the Sun, so their cycles thru all signs are close to the Sun's . . . Mars takes longer, about two years . . . Jupiter takes about 12 years to complete a full cycle thru all 12 signs. Saturn takes 28-30 years to complete a full cycle.

Because Saturn is a symbol of the wisdom which grows with age, its cycle is particularly important in reflecting our development . . . Every seven years, Saturn completes a quarter of the cycle, and we move into a new stage of awareness.

At the time of the Saturn return, when you're 28 or 29, and again in your late fifties (and again in your eighties), you have an opportunity to move into a clearer, higher, more effective level of awareness. Some people in our culture unfortunately have a lot of negative conditioning about turning 30, and about aging in general. You can let all of that negative conditioning go — there's no need for it. As we age, we grow, and deepen, and evolve.

The following is from a letter to a friend, who expressed concern and worry about her Saturn 'return' — when the cycle is completed — and about turning 30:

> *Don't give yourself any heavy or negative programming about your Saturn return – it doesn't have to be heavy at all. There's a lot of cultural neurosis about it (and about age 30 for women, and some men) – and it's all bullshit as far as I'm concerned.*
>
> *Look at it this way:*
>
> *Saturn symbolizes experience, wisdom that grows with age . . . As it returns, it has travelled thru every sign, and every house – every realm of human experience. So the Saturn return is a deep initiation, where you move to a new level of understanding, and see your life in a much broader, deeper perspective. Your Great Work becomes clearer, your work in the world becomes more focused and far more abundantly rewarding, on spiritual and material levels . . .*
>
> *Happy re-birthday*

Sit with these Symbols

Sit with these symbols

And remember this:

the 'unevolved', the 'evolving', and the 'evolved' are, actually, one and the same...

they are not tools for separating, for creating distinctions between things ... they are tools for unifying, uniting on the deepest levels

on a rational mind level, there are many separations...

on a heart level, an intuitive level, there are none...

not that we should reject rational mind: it too has its wisdom, its function... it is a tool, like astrology, to use skillfully

with heart and mind in perfect balance...

Embracing All

Here is a valuable meditation: an exercise in accepting, loving all the signs.

First, relax ... then:

Approach any sign, in your mind's eye, especially any sign you may have difficulty with ...

Mentally visualize the sign ... think of individuals you know and/or the archetypes of the sign ...

Think of their unevolved, evolving, and evolved levels ...

Approach each sign with complete acceptance ... approach each sign with love ...

There is nothing to reject in anyone ... every one of us is living out the drama that is perfect for us ...

See that each sign is a face of God.

Each sign is a path to perfection.

Each sign leads to the vast awareness that includes all signs.

The Movement of the Planets

One of the most unusual — and ultimately useful — tools for learning astrology which I have ever encountered is the 'planetary walks' which I learned from a Sufi named Abraham, a follower of the late and great Samuel Lewis, or Sufi Sam. He taught astrology in a way that interests me — as a tool for effective personal development, for growth, for evolution.

Sufi Sam taught that you could learn astrology *physically*, thru your movements . . . You can act out the energy of each planet, and by doing so, you can more deeply understand the energies these planets represent.

Each planet has its own unique energies, and we can express them, and even *summon* them, when necessary, thru physical movements. The walks are begun by simply walking around in a large circle — either alone or with a group.

Just walk 'normally' at first, fairly slowly and relaxed. Then, concentrate on one of the planets, and begin to move in ways that feel connected to that planet's particular energies . . . Soon you will start feeling that planet's natural 'energy pathway'. It is a definite energy which you can feel, which you create. And you can summon it when you wish.

The Sun Walk ☉

To do the Sun walk, let your walk become strident, strong, 'sunny' — very bright. You'll naturally feel your speed increasing somewhat. Center your energy in your head and shoulders and heart — high, clear, radiant . . . Focus on your in-breath, imagining that every time you breathe in, you are filling your head and shoulders and heart — your whole being — with strength and light and openness.

The Sun walk is very good to do when you need to climb hills or stairs. Just imagine that each in-breath is lifting you up effortlessly.

The Sun is the source of our life — connect with that life force ... imitate it ... summon it... Like the Sun, let your light shine on all.

The Moon Walk ☾

The Moon walk is quiet, slower than the Sun walk, passive, deep... You walk gently, lightly, effortlessly — almost as if you're not there at all... Become totally empty, totally receptive... Focus on your out-breath, imagining that every time you breathe out, you are releasing everything you are holding onto and/or identifying with, so that you become empty and open — a vessel waiting to be filled. Create a vacuum for the inspiration of the Universe to come pouring thru.

The Moon walk is very good to do when you're walking in nature, or any environment where you want to be sensitive and receptive. Or summon the Moon's energies when you need to descend steep hills or stairs — just imagine that each out-breath is propelling you lightly and safely downwards.

The Moon is a symbol of our 'subconscious', our connection with everyone and with all information in the universe... Let yourself become empty, and you will be filled...

The Mercury Walk ☿

The five walks which follow are those of the five ancient planets, from Mercury to Saturn. They chronicle, on one level, the life of a man or woman, from childhood to old age.

The Mercury walk is fast, active, childlike ... moving quickly, with winged heels ... moving with the speed of thought ... very often changing the focus of attention, like a young child...

Mercury has a high, bright mental activity. You can summon

Mercury energy if you want or need to write, or study, or communicate clearly and easily. You can summon Mercury energy to assist you with your creative projects, and even to help your friends with their creative dreams (see Israel Regardie's brilliant little book, *The Art of True Healing* for more information on this).

The Venus Walk ♀

Now we slow down again, in order to summon the energy of Venus. Venus is the adolescent who has just realized that she is beautiful. The walk is similar in many ways to the Moon walk, yet there is an ego in the Venus walk, an awareness of self, which is not present in the Moon's walk.

This walk is magnetic, attractive, and truly powerful ... and yet it is also innocent, radiating the world's love. Sometimes people will naturally get into a Venus walk when they "fall in love." Venus has an open heart, embracing all in her abundant love.

The Mars Walk ♂

Mars is the macho young man, aggressive, strong, creative, potentially violent if held back ... Put your mind in your third chakra ('hara' or belly) and concentrate the energy of your walk there. Become centered, powerful. You can summon a huge amount of physical energy from your legs and stomach area — the so-called "lower centers."

Mars energy is useful to summon when you have heavy work to do, especially if you have to lift or carry heavy things. It is also good to connect with if you're feeling weak or debilitated, or if in some way you have given your natural, personal power away to someone or something. Take back your power! You are free to express yourself in a huge variety of creative ways!

The Jupiter Walk ♃

With the Jupiter walk, we move into middle age — a time of growth, expansion without limits ... a time of abundance ...

Let your steps become larger, more solid, more assertive. Now that you have been given the energy of the Mars walk, feel your aura — and your whole body — expanding, growing larger and larger . . . Become huge and powerful and successful by summoning the energies of Jupiter to you, and by radiating this energy out into the world . . .

Feel your walk become stately, confident . . . the stride of Jupiter, the powerful leader.

Call forth Jupiter energy when you want to increase your abundance, or your productivity, or your successful business management capabilities, or your generosity.

The Saturn Walk ♄

Saturn is a symbol of the old person . . . Let your walk slow down . . . let your mind deepen . . . Saturn goes beyond Jupiter in its understanding: Saturn understands the nature of limits, such as time, gaining in wisdom and insight as s/he grows very old . . .

Let your walk become slow, and gentle, and profound. You are preparing to leave this physical body, to expand into a far greater body, symbolized by the outer planets . . .

The Uranus Walk ♅

Now we move beyond the physical stages, into the transcendental energies of the outer planets . . .

The walk which reflects the energies of Uranus is fast, explosive, changeable, never staying in any one rhythm too long — as soon as a pattern is established, it is shattered by the spontaneous, ever-changing energy of Uranus. Put your attention on the crown of your head — your seventh chakra — and be free and spontaneous, doing whatever you have the energy to do . . .

Experience the 'crazy wisdom' which many Tibetan Buddhist teachers speak of. Uranus is the first walk in this series which shatters the form of walking around in a circle — move in any direction, any way, fast or slow...

Let your spirit soar...

The Neptune Walk   ♆

We slow down again for the Neptune walk, for the energy of Neptune is calm and clear, centered and all-seeing... Focus your attention upon your 'third eye', between your brows (your sixth chakra) ... become quiet and receptive ... and realize that you are a visionary, a psychic, connected with your own higher intelligence, your greater being.

Just walk slowly, and focus inwardly.

The Pluto Walk   ♇

The energy of the planet Pluto is a quantum leap beyond Uranus and Neptune, just as they were a quantum leap beyond the inner planets. The Sufis teach that the energy of Pluto is too far out (literally) to be expressed within the physical form of the walks, and so they sit in a circle and chant a mantra in order to reflect Pluto's energy, such as:

Gaté, gaté, paragaté,
parasamgaté, Bodhi, Swaha!

which I've attempted to translate as follows (borrowing heavily from Allen Ginsberg):

Gone, gone, gone beyond going,
really gone! See the light!
So it is!

Song of the Planets

The following words were written to accompany these planetary walks... The words are my impressions of the planets... I hope they will convey the feeling of the energy pathway of each planet to the reader.

Sun energy!

Shining radiance!
High flowing power
     of the day's light
Stride of the Sun
Lord of Life
Lord of the Day

Into our right nostrils
     thru our right side
     flows the ever-present yang energy
          of the Universe

Inhale pure energy!
Inhale pure light!
     We are pure energy
     We are pure light!

This energy flows thru us,
     dissolving all imagined
          impurities
The Sun's fire purifies us

And we flow with high praise
     in your energy pathway —

Salute to the Sun!
Shining radiance!

Wonder of the Moon...

☾

We feel your energy
    deep within

Exquisite reflection
The Sun's golden majesty unites
    with his silver lover:
    Divine pure emptiness!
    The Mother of us all
        Queen of the night

Quiet walk of the Moon —
    quiet, like a cat
From out of our left nostrils,
    exhaling,
    flows the ever-present
    ever-empty yin-ness
        of the Universe

We are pure emptiness
        pure space
        pure energy

This energy flows thru us, deeply
    dissolving all imagined ego
        all imagined personality
        all imagined creation

And we flow blissfully
    in your energy pathway
    effortlessly flowing
        in emptiness

Moonwalk wonder
        shimmering emptiness...

Winged Mercury!

Fleet of foot, fast as thought
Speedy child, Messenger of Gods
Winged Mercury energy
Ever-changing QuickSilver
Wonder of our minds!
    Instant connection
        with the All
    Instant creation
        with the speed of thought

Rapid wind-walk of Mercury
    hiding the secrets of Hermes
        the Trickster
    here in a flash
        shimmering

Mercury —
    the ancient strength
        of mankind —
    his fleet-thinking mind —
    connection at the speed
        of light!

Sweet Venus,

Beautiful lover,
Divine Shakti,
Your walk so flowing   ♀
Your energy so bright
Your eternal adolescent
        wonder-sparkle,
        knowing you are beautiful
        knowing you are loved
            for you are Love

Sweet Venus,
Shakti of everyone,
Lover of all
        Exquisite heart energy
        Exquisite orgasm energy

        One with the Universe
            thru your Love

        thru your mantra —

        'Love me ... love me ... love me...
        'Love you ... love you ... love you...
        'Love ... love ... love...'

Mars energy!

Strapping, street-fighting Mars
Young and hot
Yang unleashed
Erect and powerful
    the force of creation!
Energy in lingam!
Energy in belly!
2nd and 3rd chakras ablaze
    with fire!

There is a war to be waged
    Demons to be conquered
Let flaming red energy
      rage!

Eternally strong —
    what can destroy him?
No thought, pure action
      Roar!

    Mars energy pathway . . .

He too is One with the Universe
      thru his lust —
    Union with yoni
Deep into the ecstasy of it All

Jupiter!

Ever-growing,
Never knowing
        anything of limits
Huge belly, huge body
Filling the space with
        positive vibrations
Showering all with his generosity

♃

Jovial Jupiter walk,
        the Santa Claus of the solar system
So big! Almost a star!
        Bigger and bigger! Ever onward!
        Ever fortunate, ever lucky
            Royal purple power!

Such joy in his walk!
The Universe is absolutely
            perfect!

Effortless energy pathway
        of eternal expansion

Saturn...   ♄

Old and silent, slow and wise,
    carefully seeing all
Your body has known pain now,
    You are shrunken...
        Father Time...

Saturn carefully looks
    and so he sees
        the wisdom of the Ancients
            the wisdom of age
        the purpose of order
            the meaning of balance
            the need for limits

   ... and so he is a Master

Old and silent, slow and wise,
    the energy pathway
        to understanding

Uranus explosion!

Crown chakra unites with the
    Universe!
Wild Aquarius energy
    crying joyously   ♅
"We're all in the 7th center
    of consciousness
        all the time!"

        7th chakra!
        7th heaven!

If there is a constant rhythm
        it is shattered —
    Ever new forms
        beyond this form
    Beyond our bodies
        We are pure energy!

    Leaping, spinning, changing,
    stopping, leaping, slowing,
    changing, spinning, stopping,
    changing . . .

Minds blown!
        Jubilance!
                Crazy wisdom
    Shatter all models!

Infinite energy pathways!

Deep Neptune

Ψ

Deep, dark-blue ocean
    of consciousness

    Sage of Space

The chakra of the 3rd eye
    All-seeing, all-knowing

      calm and clear

Deep blue of infinity
    Beyond duality

The energy is focused
    between the brows
    (Neptune's trident — Shiva's mark!)
    and then

    We see with clearer eyes
      beyond mortal eyes
        into space
    into centerlessness

    we are pure energy
      pure light

    calm and clear

deep blue of infinite . . .

Pluto

ℙ

Beyond words

Gaté Gaté Paragaté
Parasamgaté
Bodhi
Swaha!

Gone, gone, gone beyond going,
Really gone
See the light!
So it is!

The Days of the Week

Most people aren't even aware of the fact that the days of the week are named after different planets — and have been since ancient times. It is my feeling that there is a deep significance to this — a deep understanding which gives us a great deal of information about the nature of each day:

Saturday is Saturn day, a good day for growth, accomplishment.

Sunday is Sun day, a good day for rejuvenation, for high, positive relations with others.

Monday is Moon day, a good day to relax, go within. Often there is emotion ('blue Mondays') — and it is *not* the ideal day to begin your work week.

Tuesday is Mars day ('Mardi' in French), a good day for work, physical activity, creative ideas. Watch out for ego conflicts.

Wednesday is Mercury day ('Mercredi' in French), a very good day for mental work, communication, taking care of business, writing, visiting, meetings.

Thursday is Jupiter day or 'Thor's day' (the Nordic Jupiter), usually an expansive, high day, good for growth, creativity, very positive encounters with others.

Friday is Venus day ('Venerdi' in Italian), which is, as we all know from high school, great for romance and love relationships... Also good for artistic expression and settling difficulties.

Each day has its own unique energy. Tune into it — notice your feelings each day of the week and see if you experience a recurring pattern. If you do, an awareness of that pattern could be very useful in planning your activities...

The Circle of Life

Every sign has its own special
        perfection,

Just as every season of the year
        has its own perfect place.

Each sign, each season,
        has its own teachings,
        its own strengths,
        its own perfection.

The seasons, and the signs,
        are all integral parts of
        a whole, magical cycle...
        the cycle of the year,
        the cycle of life.

They're each a part of the Mandala...
        part of the Medicine Wheel...
        that is our Universe,
        that is us.

This is the circle of life.

A Simple Method of Casting a Chart

There are many different ways to cast a chart — though they are all doing basically the same thing: locating the positions of the planets, including the sun and moon and other "special points" in the heavens at someone's time of birth, or at any time you are interested in, for that matter.

When I first learned to cast charts, it involved about three hours of work, and calculated the position of the planets to the *second* (each degree of the chart consists of 60 minutes; each minute consists of 60 seconds). After several years of this, I finally realized that it was totally unnecessary to bother to be so accurate — calculating to the degree is perfectly adequate, for almost any purpose. Now I use a much simpler, faster method, which I'll give you in the following pages.

First I will go thru the steps in a general way, and then again in a more specific way, actually casting a chart. Your first chart may take you a couple of hours, but after some practice, you should be able to cast a complete chart with this method in 30 to 45 minutes.

Tools you will need

- An atlas or map of the U.S., or world, which allows you to easily locate the latitude of the place where the person was born.
- A book: *Tables of Midheavens and Ascendants*, available from your local metaphysical bookstore, or from American Federation of Astrologers, PO Box 22040, Tempe, Arizona 85282. Cost: $5.90.
- An *Ephemeris*, or table of planetary positions, for the year you are considering. Available at metaphysical bookstores, or from The Rosicrucian Fellowship, Ocean-

side, Calif. 92054.
— A blank horoscope chart. You can make your own, or
pick them up at a metaphysical bookstore, or get mine
thru Whatever Publishing (PO Box 3073, Berkeley, Calif.
94703 — 15 cents each plus postage).

Optional:

— A table of houses, if you wish to use the most common
house system (I don't use it personally, but most people
do).
— An assortment of colored pens or pencils. I feel the charts
gain much more depth when color is used, because different colors have different frequencies, which correspond to the different kinds of energies of each sign and
planet and 'special point'. I like to use red for the fire
signs, brown for the earth signs, light blue for the air
signs, dark blue for the water signs, gold or orange for
the sun, silver or blue for the moon, light blue for Mercury, green or turquoise for Venus, red for Mars, purple
for Jupiter, brown or grey for Saturn, orange for Uranus,
deep blue for Neptune, black for Pluto . . . Change those
colors, if you feel like it — use what feels right for you. I
like color because people intuitively interpret it, without
going thru rational mind words.
— *Time Changes in the USA*, and *Time Changes in the World*,
which allow you to find whether standard time or daylight savings time was in effect. Most libraries have this
information, too.

To cast a chart for any day, any time in which you're interested:

First of all, either draw or buy a blank chart. It is basically just a circle, with 360°, divided into 12 houses, each of 30°.

Then, write down this information: date, time, place. You will need to know all three of these things to cast a complete chart.

Calculating the house cusps

Turn to your atlas or map, locate the latitude. (Latitude runs horizontally around the earth; longitude runs vertically. For a simple chart, we don't even have to bother with longitude.) Make a note of the latitude.

Pick up the *Table of Midheavens and Ascendants*. Open to the date you are considering. A typical page looks like this (though this is highly reduced):

HOUR A.M.	S.T. h.m.	M.C.	Ascendant at Latitude North										
			5°	10°	20°	25°	30°	35°	40°	45°	50°	55°	60°
0000	2 36	♉ 11	♌ 8	♌ 10	♌ 13	♌ 14	♌ 16	♌ 18	♌ 20	♌ 21	♌ 24	♌ 26	♌ 28
0100	3 36	26	23	24	26	28	29	♍ 0	♍ 1	♍ 3	♍ 4	♍ 6	♍ 8
0200	4 36	♊ 11	♍ 8	♍ 9	♍ 10	♍ 11	♍ 12	12	13	14	15	16	17
0300	5 36	24	24	24	24	25	25	25	25	25	26	26	26
0400	6 37	♋ 8	♎ 10	♎ 9	♎ 9	♎ 8	♎ 8	♎ 8	♎ 7	♎ 7	♎ 7	♎ 6	♎ 6
0500	7 37	22	25	24	23	22	21	20	19	18	17	16	15
0600	8 37	♌ 7	♏ 10	♏ 9	♏ 6	♏ 5	♏ 4	♏ 3	♏ 1	30	28	26	24
0700	9 37	22	25	23	20	18	17	15	13	♏ 11	♏ 9	♏ 8	♏ 4
0800	10 37	♍ 8	♐ 9	♐ 7	♐ 3	♐ 1	29	27	25	22	19	16	13
0900	11 37	24	23	21	17	14	♐ 12	♐ 10	♐ 7	♐ 4	♐ 0	26	22
1000	12 38	♎ 10	♑ 7	♑ 5	♑ 0	28	25	23	20	16	12	♐ 7	♐ 1
1100	13 38	26	21	19	15	♑ 12	♑ 9	♑ 6	♑ 3	29	24	18	11
Noon	14 38	♏ 12	♒ 5	♒ 4	30	27	25	22	18	♑ 14	♑ 8	♑ 1	22
1300	15 38	27	21	19	♒ 16	♒ 14	♒ 12	♒ 9	♒ 5	♒ 1	25	17	♑ 6
1400	16 38	♐ 11	♓ 7	♓ 6	♓ 4	♓ 3	♓ 1	29	26	23	♒ 18	♒ 10	26
1500	17 38	25	24	24	23	22	22	♓ 21	♓ 21	♓ 19	♓ 18	♓ 14	♓ 7
1600	18 39	♑ 9	♈ 11	♈ 11	♈ 13	♈ 13	♈ 14	♈ 15	♈ 17	♈ 18	♈ 22	♈ 27	♉ 8
1700	19 39	23	28	29	♉ 1	♉ 3	♉ 5	♉ 7	♉ 10	♉ 14	♉ 19	♉ 28	♊ 11
1800	20 39	♒ 7	♉ 14	♉ 15	19	21	23	26	30	♊ 4	♊ 10	♊ 18	28
1900	21 39	22	29	♊ 1	♊ 5	♊ 7	♊ 10	♊ 13	♊ 17	21	26	♋ 3	♋ 11
2000	22 39	♓ 8	♊ 13	15	20	22	24	28	♋ 1	♋ 5	♋ 9	15	22
2100	23 39	24	27	29	♋ 3	♋ 6	♋ 8	♋ 11	14	17	21	28	♌ 1
2200	0 40	♈ 11	♋ 11	♋ 13	17	19	22	24	27	29	♌ 3	♌ 6	11
2300	1 40	27	25	27	♌ 0	♌ 2	♌ 4	♌ 6	♌ 9	♌ 11	14	17	20
2400	2 40	♉ 12	♌ 9	♌ 11	14	15	17	19	20	22	24	27	29

Find the correct 'local mean time' down the left hand side of the page, and the 'ascendant at latitude north' across the top of the page. If a person was born during Daylight Savings Time, or 'War Time' (during a World War), subtract an hour to get the 'local mean time', because during those times the country arbitrarily decided to move the clock ahead an hour. (The planets, however, remained in their course, as usual.)

Locate the point where these two parts of the graph intersect. Sometimes some interpolation is necessary here. If the time, the hour (the left hand column) wasn't exactly on the hour, or the degree of latitude (the column going across the top of the page) wasn't a figure that ends in a 0 or a 5, you'll have to do a bit of simple interpolation, or averaging. In general, it's just a matter of finding the average, probable distance of travel a planet or an ascendant or midheaven goes in a particular amount of time. For each hour, at any given latitude, you can see that the Ascendant or the Midheaven (labeled 'M.C.' — after the initials of the word 'midheaven' in Latin) changed a certain number of degrees. For whatever fraction of the hour you are interested in, just assume that the Ascendant changed a proportional number of degrees. (If this is unclear to you, hang in there — when we get to actually doing a specific chart, you'll catch on.)

With the use of the table, determine the Ascendant and Midheaven (M.C.). Note the ascendant on your horoscope blank.

Now at this point, you have several different choices available to you, three of which we'll consider.

1) You can construct a chart with an 'equal house system', which means a chart in which each of the houses have 30°. To do this, you simply put in the sign and degree which you calculated for the ascendant on your horoscope blank at the ascendant — the cusp of the 1st and 12th houses. It is almost always at the 9 o'clock position, the 'eastern horizon' of the chart. Then, you fill in each of the subsequent house cusps with the same degree of the next sign of the Zodiac, so that each house consists of 30°. (So if the Ascendant is 14° Aries, the 2nd house cusp is 14° Taurus,

the 3rd house cusp is 14° Gemini, and so on.) This is a very fast and convenient house system.

2) You can cast the chart the way I do, with a modified equal house system which places the Midheaven in the proper position — at the very top of the chart (12 o'clock position). If you tried the 'equal house system', you noticed that the midheaven (which you calculated from the *Table of Midheavens and Ascendants*) was usually not in the actual midheaven position, which is the cusp, or line, between the 9th and 10th houses. I like to put the Ascendant in its actual place and the Midheaven in its actual place, and then divide the houses equally between them. The end result is always a perfectly symmetrical chart.

For example, if the Ascendant is 5° Aries and the Midheaven is 20° Capricorn, the chart loses 15° from the Midheaven to the Ascendant — instead of 90° (a perfect quarter of a circle), we have only 75° for that quarter of the chart. So I divide each house between the Midheaven and the Ascendant equally — in this case, they'd each have 25°, instead of the 30° houses of the equal house system. But then in the next quarter of the chart, from the Ascendant to the Nadir (opposite the Midheaven, at the bottom of the chart), we gain back our 15°, because the Nadir is always exactly opposite the Midheaven. In our example, then, with the Ascendant at 5° Aries, the Nadir would be 20° Cancer, making a total of 105° for the three houses (remember, each sign has 30° in it, regardless of the number of degrees in any particular house). So the first, second, and third houses would each have 35°.

So we can calculate all the houses as follows: If the Ascendant is 5° Aries and the Midheaven is 20° Capricorn, the 10th house cusp (ie, Midheaven) is 20° Capricorn; the 11th house cusp is 15° Aquarius; the 12th house cusp is 10° Pisces; the 1st house cusp (ie, Ascendant) is 5° Aries; the 2nd house cusp is 10° Taurus; the 3rd house cusp is 15° Gemini. The other six house cusps are exactly the same number of degrees as their opposites: the 4th house cusp or Nadir (opposite the Midheaven) would be 20° Cancer; the 5th house cusp (opposite the 11th house) would be 15° Leo; the 6th house cusp (opposite the 12th house) would be 10° Virgo; the 7th house cusp (opposite the Ascendant) would be

87

5° Libra; the 8th house cusp (opposite the 2nd house) would be 10° Scorpio; the 9th house cusp (opposite the 3rd house) would be 15° Sagittarius.

3) A third and more common method of calculating the house cusps is called the Placidian system. For this, you need a table of houses. The most common is available from the same people who put out the most common Ephemeris — The Rosicrucian Fellowship, Oceanside, Calif., 92054. Another excellent table of houses is Dalton's *Table of Houses*. Each table of houses has clear instructions for its use, so I won't bother to repeat it here.

Calculating planetary positions

Now we have calculated the house cusps, and filled them in on our horoscope blank. The next, and most important, step is to calculate and fill in the positions of the planets. For this, we need our Ephemeris — our table of planetary positions.

Open your Ephemeris to the year and the date in which you are interested. For each day, the position of every planet has been calculated. Usually, it is given in 'Greenwich Mean Time', for either 12 noon or 12 midnight. This is the time in Greenwich, England. Conceivably, an Ephemeris could be calculated for each time zone, and for each hour of the day, or even each minute of the day, but the bulk of the volume would be enormous. So, we are given the positions for a certain hour and a certain place — Greenwich, England — and we have to do a bit of interpolation to find the time and place we are interested in.

First of all, let's do the place. Greenwich is 5 hours ahead of the East Coast (Eastern Standard Time), 6 hours ahead of the Midwest (Central Standard Time), 7 hours ahead of the Rockies (Mountain Standard Time), and 8 hours ahead of the West Coast (Pacific Standard Time). So we have to add that many hours to the local time we're interested in to come up with the Greenwich Mean Time which our Ephemeris is using. For example, say your friend Sally was born at 9 pm Pacific Standard Time. You have to figure that at 9 pm on the West Coast, it is actually 8 hours *later* in Greenwich (because they're ahead of us in time —

the sun passes over England first, and then America). So, 9 pm Pacific Standard Time is the same as 5 am the following day Greenwich Mean Time. Got it? If you were born at noon in New York City, you were born at 5 pm Greenwich Mean Time.

All right, so you calculate for Greenwich Mean Time. Then the only other tricky thing to do is to interpolate between the times given in the Ephemeris and the time you are looking for. Let's take your friend Sally again. Say she was born on October 1, 1970, at 9 pm Pacific Standard Time. Open your Ephemeris to that date. We've already calculated that she was born on October 2, 1970 at 5 am Greenwich Mean Time. Look at the Ephemeris. Times are given for either noon or midnight. Let's say you have a Rosicrucian Ephemeris, like I do, which gives the time for 12 noon, Greenwich Mean Time. So you have before you the planetary positions at 12 noon on October 1 and 12 noon on October 2. Our task, then, is to calculate the planetary positions for 5 am on October 2. Interpolating always just boils down to taking a simple fraction between two given pieces of information. The sample I've happened to choose, 5 am, is actually a fairly tricky fraction — you have to figure based on the 24 hours from noon to the next noon, so 5 am would be 15/24 of the way between the two. Right? For this kind of calculating, a pocket calculator is very convenient.

Here's a simpler example, to start with: say your Aunt Mergetroid was born at 2 pm in Podunk Iowa — which is Central Standard Time. That's 8 pm Greenwich Mean Time (2 + 6, right?). So in our noon-to-noon Ephemeris, we're dealing with a fraction of 8/24 or 1/3. (I feel that you don't have to be too exact about this fraction — half an hour or even an hour doesn't make too big a difference in the positions of the planets. The Moon — fastest moving planet — moves only an average of about 12° a day, taking 2½ days in the average to move thru one sign. That's only ½ of a degree an hour. The Rising Sign, on the other hand, moves a whole degree every 4 minutes — going an entire round of 360° in 24 hours — so it's much more important to calculate the Ascendant carefully — which we did, earlier.)

Now notice that, in the Ephemeris, planetary positions are given in degrees and minutes of each sign. All you have to do is approximate the number of degrees and minutes which correspond to the fraction you have calculated. A pocket calculator is very nice — but for years, I just multiplied it out by hand.

First, let's look at the Sun. Notice that, for any given period of 24 hours, the Sun moves just about 60 minutes (or from about 57-63 minutes) — just about 1 ° per day, or 360° in a full year. Does that make sense? Now for your aunt Mergetroid, born at 8 pm Greenwich Mean Time, we simply have to figure ⅓ of 60°, or 20°. Let's take a specific example. Say Mergetroid was born at 2 pm Central Standard Time on Dec. 1, 1935. We've already seen that this time is equal to 8 pm Greenwich Mean Time — in other words, when it is 2 pm in Iowa, it is 8 pm in Greenwich, England. According to my Rosicrucian Fellowship Ephemeris, the Sun was at 8°22' Sagittarius on Dec. 1 and 9°23' on Dec. 2. So in that 24-hour interval, it moved 1°1' — 1 degree and 1 minute, or 61 minutes. One-third of 61 minutes is 20⅓ minutes. I just round that off to the closest minute — that's close enough for any interpretation. Add those 20 minutes to the first day's position of 8°22', and you have found your aunt Mergetroid's Sun Sign to be 8°42' Sagittarius. Got it?

Now just do the same thing with each planet: find how much it moved in the 24-hour time span, and find, in Mergetroid's case, ⅓ of the number of degrees and minutes it moved in those 24 hours, and add that to the first to come up with the exact position of the planets at Mergetroid's birth.

Let's look at the Moon, the fastest travelling 'planetary' body. The Moon moves an average of 12° per day (so that in a month, 30 days, it travels 30 × 12 or 360° — one entire trip around the Zodiac). On Mergetroid's birthday, the Moon went from 14°53' Aquarius at Noon in Greenwich on Dec. 1, to 28°48' Aquarius at Noon the following day. (With a name like Mergetroid, I *thought* she'd have an Aquarius Moon . . .). So it travelled almost 14° that day, or, to be more exact, 13°55'. One-third of that is approximately ⅓ of 14° or 4⅔°. Add that 4°40' to 14°53', and you get 18°93', or 19°33'. That's a close enough calculation for almost any purpose. But if you're a Virgo or something, and want to be real

90

accurate, you can take exactly ⅓ of 13°55', which is ⅓ of (I'm glad I've got my pocket calculator) 13 × 60 + 55 minutes, which is ⅓ of 835 minutes, which is 278.333 minutes, which is 4°38⅓'. Add that to the original time of 14°53', and you get 18°91⅓', or 19°31⅓', which is only 1⅔ minutes away from our rough approximation, which is close enough for me . . .

And that's all there is to it. You keep using the same fraction over and over again, for every planet. (If it still isn't clear, don't worry — I'll go thru the whole thing again, when I actually do an entire chart for you.)

By the time we get to the outer planets, there is very little calculating to do, because one short day makes very little difference in their very slow rate of travel. Mergetroid's Uranus, for instance, went from 2°12' Taurus retrograde ('retrograde' means apparent backward movement thru the Zodiac as seen from Earth) to 2°10', so it's got to be 2°11' Taurus retrograde. And Neptune is even slower, travelling from 16°41' Virgo on Dec. 1 to 16°42' on Dec. 2. So I'd just pick one — 16°42' is probably most accurate — but again, it doesn't make too much difference in interpretation whether it's 16°1' or 16°59', as far as I'm concerned . . .

Now look at Pluto — it travels so slowly that its position is only given at the first of each month (at least for the earlier years of the Ephemeris — in later years it is given every day). So you have to figure out the approximate distance it moved during the month to the day you're referring to. In Mergetroid's case, it's easy, because she was born on the first. For other days, interpolation is necessary. We'll do that later, with Betty's chart.

The only other positions that are necessary to calculate are the 'special points': the North and South Node of the Moon, and the Part of Fortune. The first two are easy: the North Node is given, in earlier years (for Mergetroid) at the far right in the Ephemeris, right next to Neptune. In later years, it is given, like Pluto in earlier years, for the first day of the month, and you have to interpolate. Don't worry about the minutes of the nodes — just calculating to the degree is sufficient.

The other 'special point' — the Part of Fortune — is a little tricky to calculate, and I always wait to do it until I have put all the planets in their correct positions in the chart, so I can refer to them visually.

Perhaps the Part of Fortune is totally arbitrary — but I don't really think so, based on all the charts I have done. It always proves to fall at the perfect place for the individual you're considering. (Mine, for instance, is in Pisces in the 1st house, which points to an interest in psychic things and 'occult' things and astrology, and also shows a tendency to want to share these things with others . . .) The way in which it is calculated is supposed to go back to ancient methods, methods the Gypsies used. The formula for the Part of Fortune is as follows: the Part of Fortune is the same distance from the Ascendant (or Rising Sign) as the Moon is from the Sun.

Let's take our favorite aunt Mergetroid as an example. We have discovered that her Sun is 8°42' Sagittarius, and her Moon is 19°31' Aquarius. We haven't calculated her Ascendant yet, but at 2 pm in Podunk Iowa (latitude about 42° North — I couldn't find Podunk on my map so I'm just approximating) on Dec. 1 in my *Tables of Midheavens and Ascendants*, I find her Ascendant to be 18° Aries (no wonder she has flaming red hair!) . . . Now we have all the information necessary to calculate her Part of Fortune, which is supposed to show where her *true* fortune will lie . . . The following calculation may seem complicated, but keep in mind the fact that 1° equals 60', and each sign has 30° . . . Okay?

The distance from Mergetroid's Moon to the Sun is from 19°31' Aquarius to 8°42' Sagittarius — or, two complete signs (each 30°) plus the distance from 19°31' to 8°42' — which is 11° minus 11' (the way I'd figure it — you may figure it differently, but you should come up with the same answer), which is 10°49'. (The other way to figure it is as follows: 19°31' to 8°42' is the same as 18°91' to 8°42'. Subtracting them, you get 10°49'.)

So Mergetroid's Part of Fortune is 10°49', plus two complete signs (or 60°) from her Ascendant, in the same direction that the Moon is from the Sun . . . Her Ascendant, at 18° Aries, is the same as 17°60' Aries . . . Subtracting to get the Part of Fortune, we get 17°60' Aries minus 2 signs (Pisces, Aquarius) minus 10°49', which equals 7°11' Aquarius . . . So, Mergetroid's Part of Fortune is at 7°11' Aquarius (no wonder she is so far out!) . . .

Aspects

Now we have cast the chart. The only other thing to include is the aspects, or the connections between the planets. I am only concerned with the major aspects: conjunctions, trines, oppositions, and sextiles. There are many different kinds of minor aspects, but I feel that they are minor indeed, and I don't use them — we are given plenty of information with the houses, planets, signs, and major aspects.

Incidentally, I happen to feel that there actually may be a concrete, provable scientific explanation for the ways in which we interpret the aspects — though we are probably several years from discovering it . . . We all know the effects of a full moon — that is the power of the 'opposition', where two opposite yet complementary signs have planetary energies that are 180° from each other. And the trine aspect, which is always considered so powerful and beneficial, is when two planets are 120° from each other. If there happens to be three planets in alignment, each approximately 120° from each other, they form a 'grand trine', or an equilateral triangle. This actually forms a pyramid, with 60° angles — and it has the power of a pyramid. I feel that soon, some bright physicist is going to come up with an explanation of the kind of energy that a pyramid (with 60° angles) generates, or rather, channels. And that explanation may very well apply to trine aspects in astrology too.

I like to interpret the aspects relatively tightly. Some astrologers interpret them so loosely that everyone's chart is filled with dozens of aspects. Four degrees of variance from the exact angle is maximum for the planets, I feel, in considering them in an aspect; five degrees for the Moon, and six or at most seven degrees for the Sun (though some astrologers will go up to 12° for the Sun).

♂   Here's an easy way to calculate the aspects: **Conjunctions** are between planets in the same sign, or right on the cusp of two different signs, within 4° of each other (or 5° if the Moon is involved, or 6° or at most 7° if the Sun is involved).

✳   **Sextile** aspects (60° apart) are between planets that are exactly two signs away from each other, plus or minus 4° (or 5° for Moon, 6° for Sun). For example: the Sun at 20° Aries is sextile Mercury at 14° Gemini, and also sextile Venus at 24° Aquarius.

□   **Square** aspects (90° apart) are between planets that are three signs away from each other, plus or minus 4°... For example: the Sun at 20° Aries is squared Mars at 15° Cancer, and Jupiter at 22° Capricorn.

△   **Trine** aspects (120° apart) are between planets that are four signs away from each other, plus or minus 4°... For example: Mercury at 22° Libra is trine Mars at 18° Gemini.

☍   Opposite aspects, or **oppositions**, (which do not necessarily always denote 'opposition') are 180° or six signs apart, plus or minus 4°. For example, that Sun at 20° Aries would be opposite Uranus at 17° Libra.

I like to draw in the planets in colored pencil (I mentioned the colors I use earlier — gold or orange for Sun, silver or blue for Moon, light blue for Mercury, green for Venus, red for Mars, purple for Jupiter, brown for Saturn, orange for Uranus, deep blue for Neptune, black for Pluto), and then connect the ones that are in relationship to each other, aspected to each other, in colored pencil, too. I usually use a dotted green line for the sextiles, a red line for both the squares and oppositions, a green line for the trines, and a little green bracket or something for the conjunctions.

Using those colors, you can interpret the aspects by relating it to a stoplight: when there's a green light, the energy is flowing, and you can easily cross the street. When there's a red light, or, in this case a red line, there's some kind of blocked energy or obstacle — which is always a message from the universe, a teaching, an opportunity to look at yourself, see where you're holding back, and grow.

We've now cast the entire chart. The last step I always do is to list "Earth - Air - Fire - Water" and "Creating - Sustaining - Changing" somewhere on the chart, and to list each planet there. It gives you a quick glance at how many planets are in Earth signs, how many are in Changing signs, etc. For example: if the person has their Sun in Taurus, Mercury in Pisces, I'd put a little symbol for the Sun after "Earth," and again after "Sustaining" — because Taurus is a Sustaining Earth sign. And I'd put a little symbol for Mercury after "Water" and after "Changing," because Pisces is a Changing Water sign.

In case you don't know, the signs, beginning with Aries, Taurus, etc., are in a regular progression of Fire sign, Earth sign, Air sign, Water sign ... and also in a regular progression of Creating sign, Sustaining sign, Changing sign. So, every sign of the Zodiac is a unique combination of an element — fire, earth, air, or water — and a type of energy — creating, sustaining, or changing. Just tuning into these two qualities can give you a lot of information in interpretation.

Here's the complete list:
Aries: Creative Fire
Taurus: Sustaining Earth
Gemini: Changing Air
Cancer: Creative Water
Leo: Sustaining Fire
Virgo: Changing Earth
Libra: Creative Air
Scorpio: Sustaining Water
Sagittarius: Changing Fire
Capricorn: Creative Earth
Aquarius: Sustaining Air
Pisces: Changing Water

In the old days, incidentally, they called the three stages of energy *"cardinal, fixed and mutable."* You can use those words if you like, but it took me about six years to realize what they were talking about. I finally understood when I first heard of "Brahma the Creator, Vishnu the Preserver, Shiva the Destroyer" in the Hindu religion. They represent the same three forces of the universe — the stages that every created thing must go thru.

I place the 'special points' more toward the center of the chart, and the planets toward the outer edge — that way, I keep them separate. I use purple for both the North Node of the Moon and the Part of Fortune, and black for the South Node.

Now, our chart is cast.

Casting a Sample Chart

Now we're ready to take an actual date, time, and place and cast an actual chart. Then we'll do the interpretation. Let's take this as a sample:

> Betty Morr
> March 11, 1934
> 1:05 pm EST (Eastern Standard Time)
> Camden, New Jersey

First of all, note that the time given was Eastern Standard Time. If it had been Eastern Daylight Time, or War Time, we would have had to subtract an hour, and calculate this chart for 12:05 pm, because time is moved ahead during daylight savings time and war time.

Now turn to your atlas or map. Find Camden, New Jersey, and write down the approximate latitude. According to my little *Hammond World Atlas*, Camden New Jersey is just about 40° N. latitude.

Now we're ready for the *Table of Midheavens and Ascendants*. Open to the page closest to March 11, which is March 10. (The pages, you will notice, are given every three days. If the day you are considering is not listed, find the one closest to it.) Go down the left hand side of the page to 1 pm (or '1300'). From there, go over to the right to the latitude of the ascendant which you are considering — in this case 40°. The figure given is 21° Cancer. Now we need to do a slight bit of interpolation, because the birthtime was 1:05, not 1:00, and the date was March 11, not March 10. For each additional four minutes of time, the ascendant moves 1° forward. So we would add 1° to that 21° Cancer to get 22° Cancer. And for each day, each number on the chart increases by 1°, so add another degree for the extra day. Now take your blank chart which you've drawn up yourself or which you've bought somewhere, and fill in the Ascendant which you've just calculated: 23° Cancer. Put it on the left hand side of the chart (at the 9 o'clock position). See the chart on page 103.

Now go to the column on the same page which is headed 'MC' — these are the initials of Mid-Heaven in Latin. Note that at 1:00 pm we are given a Midheaven of 3° Aries. Again, we must add 1° for the extra 5 minutes, and another degree for the extra day. Now mark 5° Aries at the top of your chart, on the cusp of the 9th and 10th houses — the Midheaven position. We have now determined the Ascendant, or 'Rising Sign', and the Midheaven. The next step is the house cusps.

If you want to use the equal house system, simply label each house 23°. The Ascendant is 23° Cancer, so the Second House cusp is 23° Leo, the Third House cusp is 23° Virgo, and so on around the circle. Note that, with this system, you put 23° Aries in the Midheaven position, rather than the actual midheaven we calculated.

If you wish to use the Placidian system, which is the most common, get a *Table of Houses*, and follow the directions given in the front of the book.

If you wish to use a 'modified equal house system', which is the one I prefer, you'd figure it this way: The Midheaven is 5° Aries, and the Ascendant is 23° Cancer. Because there are 30° in a sign (and 30° in each house in the equal house system), we can easily figure that, in the three houses from the Midheaven to the Ascendant, we gained 18° (23−5) from the 'normal' number of 30° for each house, or 90° for the three houses. So I simply figure that each house gained a third of that, or 6°. (Sometimes you will lose a number of degrees, so you subtract the loss rather than add the gain.) So, with the Midheaven given at 5° Aries, the 11th house cusp would be 5+6, or 11° Taurus, the 12th house cusp would be 11+6, or 17° Gemini, and the Ascendant is 17+6, or 23° Cancer, which is what we have already calculated.

Now, for the next three signs, we will have to *subtract* the 6° we have added, in order to come up with the right number of degrees in the whole circle. So the 2nd house cusp is 23−6 or 17° Leo, the 3rd house cusp is 17−6 or 11° Virgo, and the 4th house cusp, or Nadir, is 11−6 or 5° Libra, which is exactly opposite the Midheaven (5° Aries), which it must be.

The remaining houses are then easily figured out by just taking the opposite sign and the same number of degrees of the house directly opposite. So the 5th house is 11° Scorpio (opposite the 11th house 11° Taurus), the 6th house cusp is 17° Sagittarius (opposite the 12th house cusp of 17° Gemini), the 7th house cusp is 23° Capricorn (opposite the Ascendant of 23° Cancer), the 8th house cusp is 17° Aquarius (opposite the 2nd house cusp of 17° Leo), and the ninth house cusp is 11° Pisces (opposite the 3rd house cusp of 11° Virgo). We have now calculated the house cusps, so fill them in on your chart.

Now we're ready for the Ephemeris — the table of planetary positions. Open it to the appropriate year and month — in this case, March, 1934. This one table will give us all the information we need.

At the top of my Ephemeris, it says "Calculated for Mean Noon at Greenwich." (*Mean* time simply means an average, calculated for the middle of the time zone. The time varies slightly in the eastern and western parts of any given time zone, but the difference is not worth worrying about, in my opinion — altho some astrologers disagree with me.) So the planetary positions given for March 11, 1934 in our Ephemeris are those that were happening at 12 noon in Greenwich England. We need to figure out how much those planets moved as observed from Camden New Jersey at 1:05 pm. New Jersey is on the East Coast, so it is five hours *behind* Greenwich England. Therefore at 1:05 pm in New Jersey, it was actually 6:05 pm in England. So, by calculating where the planets were at 6:05 in Greenwich, we will also be finding where they were at 1:05 in New Jersey. Simple, right?

In this case, we have a very simple fraction to deal with: 6:05 pm is just slightly more than one-quarter of the way from noon on one day to noon the next. Sometimes the fraction is much more difficult, like 11/24, or 7/48 — in those cases a pocket calculator is very handy.

Look on the Ephemeris for the correct day — in this case the 11th. Notice that the Sun is given as 20°14' (20 degrees, 14 minutes) Pisces. The following day, it is given as 21°14' Pisces. So during the course of one day, 24 hours, the sun travelled exactly 1°, or 60'. So, during the first six hours, or one-quarter of that time, the sun travelled ¼ of 60°, or 15°. So we simply add that 15° to the original time of 20°14', and we have found the position of the Sun to be 20°29' Pisces. That's all there is to it — now we simply have to do the same calculation for each of the planets.

The Moon was at 26°38' Capricorn on the 11th of March, and 11°05' Aquarius on the 12th. So it travelled 14°27' over the 24-hour period. One-fourth of 14°27' is a little tricky to calculate. You can do it by just adding ¼ of 14°, which is 3.5° (or 3°30'), and ¼ of 27', which is 6.75', for a total of 3°36¾' . . . Round it off to 3°37', and add it to the original 26°38' Capricorn, and you get 29°75' Capricorn, or 30°15' Capricorn, or 0°15' Aquarius for the position of the Moon. (Keep in mind that there are 30° per sign, yet there are 60' per degree.)

The Sun and the Moon are the most difficult to calculate — after that, they get progressively easier, because they move far less (from our perspective here on Earth, anyway . . .).

Next, we look at Mercury, and we see that it apparently moved backwards, or went "retrograde." At noon on the 11th, it was at 9°33' Pisces; on the 12th, it was at 8°48' Pisces. So its apparent motion in our skies over the 24-hour period was *backward* 45'. One-quarter of this is 11.25. Subtracted from the original, we arrive at 9°22' Pisces for the position of Mercury. (Note that I round off the seconds. It is not at all necessary to be accurate to the second, just to the degree.)

Now look at Venus, and the calculations start getting easy. It moved from 11°23' Aquarius to just 11°52' Aquarius, or only 29 degrees. One-fourth of that is 7.25 degrees. So we have calculated Venus to be at 11°30' Aquarius.

Continue with Mars, Jupiter, Saturn, Uranus and Neptune in

the same way. Notice that, in earlier Ephemerides, the position of Pluto is given only for the first of each month, because its apparent motion is so minute, from our perspective. My Ephemeris gives the position of Pluto for March 1 as 22°46′ Cancer, and for April 1 as 22°30′ Cancer. So, although we aren't sure when, at some time during that month, Pluto was retrograde, or moving apparently backwards. So the best we can do is just approximate its position. At least we're sure to the degree, and that's close enough. The 11th of March is about a third of the way between the two, so I'll just guess the position of Pluto to be approximately 22°41′ Cancer. That's close enough. If you're a stickler for accuracy, find a good computer service to cast the chart.

The North Node is given in the right hand column — just round it off to the nearest degree. In later Ephemerides, the North Node is given just for the first day of the month at the bottom of the page. Calculate it roughly for the day you are interested in, and round off to the nearest degree. The North Node for this particular day is given as 17°54′ Aquarius, so we'll just round it off to 18° Aquarius. The South Node is exactly opposite, so it is at 18° Leo.

Now we come to the Part of Fortune — our last thing to calculate. I usually like to put all the planets and the nodes in the chart, using my different colors for the different planets, so I can then visually see what I'm doing as I calculate the Part of Fortune. The Part of Fortune is the same distance from the Ascendant as the Moon is from the Sun. Another way to put it is this: The distance that the Moon would take to reach the Sun is the same as the distance from the Part of Fortune to the Ascendant. Look at Betty's chart. Her Moon at 0°15′ Aquarius would have to travel 50°14′ to reach her Sun at 20°29′ Pisces. So the Part of Fortune must be 50°14′ from the Ascendant, in the same direction that the Moon is from the Sun. The Ascendant is 23° Cancer — subtracting 50° from 23° Cancer, we find ourselves at 3° Gemini. This is her Part of Fortune.

Now fill in the planets and special points on the chart, listing them in the lower left (if you use a form similar to mine) and drawing them in in their approximate place in the chart itself.

Now we're ready for the aspects. First, look at the Sun at 20° Pisces, and see if any of the other planets are within 6° of that in any of the major aspects — two signs apart, three signs apart, four signs apart, six signs apart, or conjunct, in the same sign. The only planet that is aspected to Betty's sun is Pluto, which is 22° Cancer. They are four signs apart, so they are *trine*. Now look at the Moon, at 0° Aquarius. Mars, at 27° Pisces, is almost two complete signs away (60°), so we would have to consider that a *sextile*. Look at Mercury next. With the planets, I just consider 4° off from the exact angle to be the maximum for an aspect. Mercury is almost exactly opposite Neptune, which is at 10° Virgo. This is an *opposition*. Make lines to show these aspects: Green for conjunctions, sextiles, and trines, and red for squares and oppositions.

Go thru all the planets, and find all relevant major aspects. Don't do aspects with the special points.

Now we have almost completed our chart. The only other thing I do is to fill in, in the bottom right hand corner, whether the planets (and Ascendant and Midheaven) are Earth, Air, Fire, or Water and whether they're Creating, Sustaining, or Changing.

Now the chart is complete — I sometimes put the Sun, Moon, and Rising Signs at the top, for a finishing touch, because these three are the most important factors in interpretation. Now that we've cast the chart, we'll interpret it.

A Sample Chart

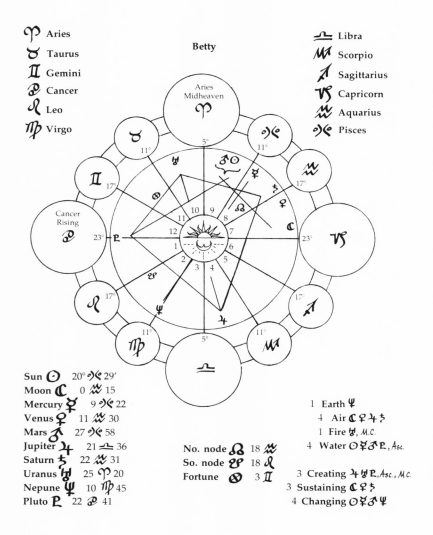

♈	Aries		♎	Libra
♉	Taurus		♏	Scorpio
♊	Gemini		♐	Sagittarius
♋	Cancer		♑	Capricorn
♌	Leo		♒	Aquarius
♍	Virgo		♓	Pisces

Betty

Aries Midheaven ♈

Cancer Rising ♋

Sun ☉	20° ♓ 29′
Moon ☾	0 ♒ 15
Mercury ☿	9 ♓ 22
Venus ♀	11 ♒ 30
Mars ♂	27 ♓ 58
Jupiter ♃	21 ♎ 36
Saturn ♄	22 ♒ 31
Uranus ♅	25 ♈ 20
Nepune ♆	10 ♍ 45
Pluto ♇	22 ♋ 41

No. node ☊	18 ♒
So. node ☋	18 ♌
Fortune ⊗	3 ♊

1 Earth ♆
4 Air ☾♀♃♄
1 Fire ♅, M.C.
4 Water ☉☿♂♇, Asc.

3 Creating ♃♅♇, Asc., M.C.
3 Sustaining ☾♀♄
4 Changing ☉☿♂♆

103

A Sample Chart Interpretation

Before interpreting...

Before interpreting a chart, it is very good to do one thing: either silently, or aloud, ask for clear guidance from the powers that you choose to create ... from your higher self, from the divine ...

Ask, and you shall receive ...

Before I begin, I always like to say something like this — it clears the air, I feel, in a positive way:

Astrology is an intuitive science — as such, it reflects the astrologer as much as it reflects the person whose chart we're considering. It reflects where an astrologer is coming from ... It can only be as clear as the interpreter is clear ...

Every word that any astrologer, any psychic, any guru, or *anyone* says comes thru our own interpretive systems, our own 'filters', our own views of reality ... If these words are meaningful to you, if they resonate positively with your inner understanding, welcome them, accept them, use them for your growth ... But if any of these words don't feel accurate, or meaningful, or useful, then just throw them out ... don't let them have any influence over you ... (I feel this way especially when interpreting aspects in a chart — especially squares and 'oppositions'.)

You are the master of your being ... you and only you really knows what in your heart is best for you ... Others can only point the way ... teachers or gurus can only point within you ...

The truth is within you ...

The intuitive science and artform and game of astrology, properly used, is a tool for deep inner growth, for skillful and conscious living, for harmonious relationships, for happiness, balance, peace . . .

Each of the 12 signs has its own unique energy . . . its own skillful means and strength . . . its own path. It's all part of the beauty and bounty of the Universe . . . The purpose of interpretation, I feel, is to find your own path . . . whatever that may mean to you . . . Every person's path is different — everyone has a unique birth chart.

Each sign is a face of God . . . each of us is evolving in our own unique, individual way. Astrology, clearly used, can reflect and assist that evolution.

Now we'll look at Betty's chart in depth. The following is written directly to her — it is one of the few written interpretations I've bothered to do.

In general —

Your birth chart is a pretty accurate chart of the positions of the planets in the heavens at the time of your birth. When you were born, the constellation Cancer, the Moonchild, was rising in the East . . . Uranus, Mars, and the Sun were very close to the Midheaven, directly above you — Uranus 20° before it, and the Sun and Mars conjunct (united) 7 - 15° after the Midheaven. After them, Mercury, Saturn, Venus and the Moon spanned the entire Western sky, and the Moon is very close to setting . . . You have what is called a *stellium* of planets — a string of many of them close together . . . Seven planets are in the Midheaven and the Western sky . . . Symbolically, this means that much of your work will be in relating to the outer world, in career, and in growth, and in relationships . . .

You have only 2 planets below the horizon — below the line of the Ascendant and Descendant: Neptune and Jupiter. Pluto is exactly on your Ascendant — that is, Pluto was just rising at your moment of birth . . . I'll get more specific with all of this later, but

I just wanted to give you a general picture of the whole...

The lines I've drawn between certain planets are the 'aspects'... It is said that, when planets come into a certain relationship with each other — when they're together (conjunct) or exactly opposite ('opposition') or in 90° positions (square), or 120° from each other ('trine'), or 60° from each other ('sextile') — there is an energy that happens between them... Your aspects form a strong and striking pattern — very much like a jewel, a diamond...

It is a chart which signifies spiritual flight — every one of your Houses above the earth, in the Midheaven, has something strong in it... You have much to show the world ... much to learn, much to teach... This lifetime will be for you a lifetime of very positive, very rapid growth — leaps in consciousness ... transformation.

Let's go thru the whole chart, more specifically — thru the Houses, from 1-12. Like the signs, the houses reflect a natural progression and development — beginning with the first (the slice of the pie with the number '1' in it) and moving counter-clockwise thru all 12.

More specifically —

Cancer
Rising
At the moment of your birth the constellation Cancer was rising in the East. So that means symbolically that Cancer 'rules your first house'... The first house (and the 'Rising Sign' — the same thing) has long been correlated with physical appearance, with how you appear to the world, with your 'outermost' levels of your personality — what other people see in you ... first impressions... Cancer is ruled by the Moon — the sign has a great deal of depth (like all water signs) and psychic openness ... a great deal of receptiveness and sensitivity...

With Cancer Rising, there's a very good chance

that other people see you as warm and loving and sensitive... People naturally trust you and rely on your intuition... You are a good teacher... You may tend to be quiet and passive in some circumstances — that's okay, that's very beautiful in fact (I'm a Cancer myself, and I'm totally biased in their favor...). Cancer is the sign of the Mother — other people may really see you as a loving Mother... It is also the sign of the witch, in the highest sense of the word, divorced from Puritan and Victorian filters — 'witch' and 'wise' come from the same root word... A true witch is one who has made a connection with their deepest inner nature — symbolized by the Moon...

You may be drawn to doing quiet, simple things ... living quietly, perhaps... In whatever ways you choose to live, you will always touch people deeply, and innately give them something which they will really appreciate... And you may not even know, or be fully aware, of your contribution to the betterment of humankind in general... Like the Moon, you reflect the beauty in others, and may not even be fully aware of the beauty in you — which is there, strongly and clearly — yet it is a deep, exquisite, subtle beauty, a beauty which reflects the beauty in others, showing them that they, too, are beautiful...

With Pluto on the horizon, all of this is even deepened. We'll deal with Pluto more when we get to the end: the 12th house...

Pluto on the horizon

The Rising Sign is the natural house of Aries, the sign of the Beginning, the sign which has the natural spontaneity of a child... The Rising Sign can reflect how others see you, how you look on an outer level, even tho it may not be at all how you feel on inner levels (which the Sun Sign

107

reflects), or how you really are on deepest levels (which the Moon Sign reflects)...

With Cancer Rising, people probably see you as soft, warm, loving ... with a big heart ... whether you feel that way or not...

2nd house ruled by Leo...

Your 2nd house (the slice of the pie with the number '2' in it) is ruled by Leo... Symbolically, then, the kind of energies symbolized by Leo — fiery, outgoing, creative — are connected with the area of experience of life that the 2nd house is associated with: your grounding, resources, money, physical plane stuff (it is the natural house of Taurus). So, you have the strength and creativity to really get your material plane trip together... You probably have created a relatively abundant reality for yourself, in many ways... You have a lot to share... You are probably lucky in investments and things like that — Leo is a symbol of the Sun's energy: strong, life-giving, contributing to growth... You have many beautiful physical plane resources which you can share with the world...

...with South Node

Your 'South Node of the Moon' is in Leo in your 2nd house... This is one of the three 'special points' in your chart — points that aren't planets, but have a deep meaning nevertheless... The Moon is slightly off the central path of the ecliptic — the path of the Sun and the other planets as we see them in the heavens, rising in the East and setting in the West. The Moon crosses the ecliptic twice a day, in the North and in the South. Astrology since ancient times has felt that these points have special meaning. The South Node, like several other things in astrology (including the 12th house, the planet Saturn, and the signs of Scorpio and Pisces), is really misunderstood in most of the astrology being proliferated today . . . It is called 'the dragon's tail, your place of self-undoing', and it is usually a place to fear . . . But, in the light of New Age astrology, it is no longer a place to fear — it is a blessing . . . To the Victorian mind (or whatever you want to call it), very attached to ego, feeling very self-important (and at the same time doubting it), and believing in only this one lifetime, encountering a 'place of self-undoing' *is* a fearful thing . . . But in the light of new understanding, your 'place of self-undoing' becomes a place where you can overcome limited views of yourself, ie, *ego*. As we grow, we begin to see that our self-concepts are, on one very important level, our entire problem; because we have views of ourselves as limited beings, we are forever limited. But the South Node offers us an opportunity to break thru all limitation, to go beyond all views of ourself.

Your's is in the sign of Leo, the Performer's sign — in some ways (ruled by the Sun and all), an opposite kind of energy than your Cancer rising type of energy . . . So a place where you can discover many whole new sides of yourself is in being freely outgoing, shining your light on all, like the Sun . . . At times you may want to be an introvert, which is beautiful — but plunge into being an extrovert every once in a while, too, and you will grow immensely . . . With Pisces Sun, Cancer Rising and Aquarius Moon, you have a lot of psychic depth, a lot of inner plane activity . . . There is a season for everything — there is a time for you to express yourself, to really put it out there, to work for and enjoy your material plane accomplishments . . . And there is a time, too, to give it all up, to look within, to be alone with yourself, within yourself — for that is where all the answers actually lie . . . that is where your true treasure is . . .

The 3rd house is the natural house of Gemini, and it relates to communication — how you express yourself . . . (It also relates to brothers and sisters, short-distance travel, and mental activity . . .) Virgo rules your third house, meaning the energies symbolized by Virgo are prevalent here . . . Virgo, too, is often misunderstood in the usual forms of astrology known today . . . Virgo is really a symbol of the powers of Mercury (the Messenger of the Gods, ie, communication from divine sources, ie, our own rational minds!) brought to Earth, for the sign of Virgo is an Earth sign . . .

Virgo is often seen in its unevolved form, as negative and critical . . . But Virgo is really the power of discriminating wisdom . . . Virgo is really a Healer, a selfless servant of all . . . So, with Virgo ruling your third house, you will make a very good teacher . . . Communicative doors will open for you as you love and serve others . . . You have healing potential and ability . . .

All of this is definitely reinforced, strengthened, with the addition of the powerful outer planet Neptune right on the cusp — the imaginary line in the chart between the houses . . . Neptune is a symbol for the 6th chakra — '3rd eye' — energies . . . the energy of intuition, inner vision . . . interpenetration . . . It is a symbol for the inner sight which we all have — a high, delicate energy which we can tune into, if we wish . . . Neptune relates to the eyes with which we see our dreams — for we are not using our physical eyes when we dream — and our intuitive flashes and insights . . .

With Neptune in Virgo, you do have the capability to be a psychic or visionary healer, in some way . . . Silva Mind Control, or something else

110

which can tune you into the healer within you, would be very easy for you — it would be second nature... And, at the same time, serving others — in many ways — has some beautiful effects for you, for it can open up your inner understanding...

With Neptune bridging your 2nd and 3rd houses, this symbolically brings your deepest resources into play as you communicate the vision you see to the world...

You are a natural poet, too ... or a visionary artist, in some unique way...

The 4th house is the natural house of Cancer... The cusp of the 4th house is called the Nadir — it shows the constellation that was directly below you at birth ... the opposite of the Midheaven...

Libra rules 4th house...

The Nadir, then, is a symbol of your ground, your inner center ... the Within. Like the 8th house and the 12th house, it is a deep psychic Source... Libra rules your 4th house: Deep beauty is within! You are a natural artist, receptive and attuned...

Your natural abilities are strengthened by Jupiter's presence in Libra — for wherever Jupiter is, there radiates a very strong, positive energy, expansive and outgoing... You have many capabilities — in the arts, in relationship, in law: in everything ruled by Venus. It is always within you — your meditation will point the way to it. Anything ruling your fourth house is found by meditation — there is no need to go searching in any outward way for the teachings there — it is all within you...

... with Jupiter in Libra in 4th house

This Jupiter in the 4th house is a very positive sign: there is natural abundance within you ... Meditation will be very fruitful for you ... It will give you the key which resolves all apparent conflict: the key of *balance*.

Jupiter opposite Uranus

The red line connecting Jupiter and Uranus symbolizes an 'opposition' — meaning that the planets were 180° apart at your birth ... Traditionally they say that oppositions point to difficulties or apparent conflicts ... In an opposition that involves Jupiter and Uranus, and 4th and 10th houses, traditional astrology would say that you may have experienced some apparent conflict between your home life and your career, and/or between your inner work, your meditation, and your work in the world, your job ...

Yet New Age astrology always sees strengths in so-called oppositions — oppositions (and squares) are the perfect opportunity for growth ... they can symbolize the pain that must be felt and understood before true understanding and bliss can emerge ... The key to every opposition, to all apparent conflict, is 'balance' ... Find the perfect natural balance between your home life and your work ... between your desire for meditation and your work in the world — there is a season for everything, and you know in your heart what to do ...

Jupiter trine Saturn

The planet Saturn — symbolically, the wisdom that grows with age — is very powerfully connected with both Jupiter and Uranus ... so it is another solution to any apparent problems: the wisdom of your experience is something you can rely on ... It may present solutions that shatter your own models of how things *should* be ... but trust it ...

Scorpio is a symbol of transformation, a rich, deep symbol of the evolution of sexual energy into visionary oneness with the whole of creation . . . It is a mystical sign, and it is a very physical sign . . . It is tantra yoga . . . The 5th house is the natural house of Leo, and so it symbolizes creative expression, performing, children, outgoing things — sharing the understanding you gained on the inner planes in the 4th house with the whole world . . .

Scorpio rules 5th house

So your expression to the world might be very deep and transformative . . . You have many talents — let them shine . . .

The 6th house goes beyond the 5th house, into really applying the creative ability of the 5th house in a way that loves and serves others . . . The 6th house is the natural house of Virgo, and it deals with work, service, and healing . . . Sagittarius is ruled by Jupiter, so wherever you have Sagittarius ruling, you have an expansive capability and a natural, exhuberant understanding . . . In your work you have a healing vibration that others can feel . . . You have healing potential . . .

Sagittarius rules 6th house

Love, serve, and heal.

The 7th house, being the natural house of Libra, deals with relationships . . . and things like contracts, partnerships, etc. You have Capricorn ruling: don't take your relationships too seriously! And yet, wherever Capricorn rules you have skill and capability and clear insight — so, for you (for everyone, actually, regardless of their charts), relationships can be very deep, very beautiful teachings . . . giving you much to rapidly grow with . . . really helping you evolve quickly . . .

Capricorn rules 7th house . . .

It also means that you have business skill, when

113

you wish to tap into it ... real skill in dealing with contracts... A partnership form of business might be very rewarding...

... *with Moon & Venus in Aquarius*

Moon and Venus in Aquarius in your 7th house! How beautiful! You may have many beautiful Aquarian relationships... 'Aquarian' in many ways: New Age ... visionary possibilities ... also with elements of the unexpected, and filled with change ... wherever there's an Aquarian influence, models are shattered ... social models of how it *should* be, how it was in the past, etc., all dissolve in the new light of a higher, Aquarian understanding... A new age is dawning, change is taking place. There is nothing to reject ... everyone has their freedom, everyone has the right to do exactly as their heart tells them...

When the Moon and Venus are close together, in the same sign, there is heightened sensitivity and intuition... In Aquarius, this would show a heightened, intuitive understanding of Aquarian values and the nature of the changes that are taking place... You may be a complete romantic and idealist — beautiful! The Age of Existentialism is dead... Embrace your highest ideals... Love it all... There's no need for any guilt in any kind of relationship... There's no need for any guilt at all...

You are a sensitive, aware person... You are a very unique individual, very creative in your own way... Let yourself be...

Aquarius rules 8th house...

The 8th house is the natural house of Scorpio, and it deals with relationship taken to the deepest, mystical levels: sex and birth and death and transformation... It symbolizes, when understood, finding the keys to ultimate reality within every moment of daily life, rejecting nothing... It is the house of tantra...

Your 8th house is ruled by Aquarius, a high, visionary sign... Aquarius is a sign of spiritual nourishment... Your deepest understanding is here... Every moment can be making love ... and within making love are the deepest teachings of the universe...

You have Saturn here, your third planet in Aquarius... Saturn gains more and more strength and clarity and insight with age ... it is a symbol of the wisdom that grows with age... As you grow older, you will open out more and more effortlessly into the Aquarian ideals, and Aquarian lifestyle... You're the kind of person who will get into something totally new and challenging when you're 84 years old ... or any age...

... with Saturn...

Understanding the nature of change is a very good meditation for you — for accepting and embracing change can be a path of liberation for you...

Your North Node of the Moon is here, called the 'Dragon's Head' — your place of strength and protection... Your strength is in your ability to change ... your strength is in your understanding which grows with experience...

... & North Node in Aquarius

You have three major planets in Aquarius (as well as your 'dragon's head') — this, blended with your equally strong Piscean influences may prove to be the key to your chart: the key is in your contribution to humankind ... and it is thru your own inner growth ... thru being totally honest about where you're at, and thru loving and serving and teaching others...

Aquarius! & Pisces blended...

115

Aquarius is the humanitarian, the one committed to the Great Work, and Pisces is the Mystic . . . the one doing inner work . . . meditating, in some way . . . finding the key to the mysteries of the Universe in ways beyond daily life, beyond outer activity . . .

Let yourself be a complete idealist, if that's what you resonate with . . . Let yourself be whatever you wish . . . You are a totally unique individual . . .

Mercury,
Sun & Mars
in Pisces

You have Mercury, Sun and Mars very close together in Pisces, spanning the 8th and 9th houses — symbolically, taking the inner discoveries of the 8th house, and bringing them out, to the world . . . Mercury is the force doing this — or, *symbolizing* this, if you'd rather say it that way . . . Mercury is the Communicator of the Gods, a symbol of divine intelligence . . . a symbol of connecting with your higher self . . . Your connection is found in your most intimate, inner moments . . . in making love . . . in meditating . . . in prayer of many kinds . . . But then, this connection has to lead to a very tangible, physical expression in the world — this is what Mars conjunct the Sun suggests . . . Teaching physical education is perfect for you . . . and/or teaching yoga — some very physical expression . . . You are very connected with your body, perhaps in a very physical way that some people are not . . . and you can teach people to find this physical connection . . .

The Sun is a symbol of your life force this lifetime, and of your basic personality this lifetime . . . Mars is a symbol of the seed of creation — it is two-edged: if ego gets involved in a blind, separating way, it can lead to ego conflict and even violence . . . but when Mars energy is un-

116

derstood and used creatively, it becomes a very powerful, creative force ... a force of transformation ... This life could be a life of incredible transformation — I definitely feel it will be, in fact ...

Sun conjunct Mars in the 9th house in Pisces: This is a very rich, deep symbol — one that bears meditating with ... The 9th house is the natural house of Sagittarius, and so it is the house of growth, of expansion into the outer world, the house of infinite possibilities ... it is all the study, growth, experience and change that leads to the 10th house of material plane mastery, of 'career' ...

Sun conjunct Mars in the 9th house points to a very creative, outgoing individual ... always growing ... loving to explore and travel ...

Sun conjunct Mars in 9th house in Pisces ...

And yet, these planetary influences are coming thru the sign of Pisces: the last sign, the ultimate sign, the sign of the Mystic, the Beyond, the Christ ... It is the most *inner* sign of all.

It is my feeling that Christ had all 7 ancient planets (Sun, Moon, Mercury, Venus, Mars, Jupiter, and Saturn) all conjunct in Pisces ... So he was the supreme, the ultimate Pisces ... And so he initiated the Age of Pisces, which is now coming to an end with the dawning of the Age of Aquarius, which is initiated by the second coming of the Christ Light within *all* of us ... In the Age of Aquarius, everyone is the Avatar, everyone is tuned into their higher self ... The Age of Aquarius dawns for each person when they discover this, within themselves.

You're a wondrous
Star creation
A vessel filled with
Love and Light Divine

Aries rules
Midheaven . . .

The 10th house is the 'Midheaven' — the point directly above you at birth . . . Some astrologers say it is just as important as your Sun, Moon, and Rising signs . . .

The Midheaven relates to career, work in the world, material plane achievement and mastery . . . Your Midheaven is ruled by Aries (which is ruled by *Mars*): this points to ever-changing creative potential with your work in the world . . . You're very good at getting things started . . . you could probably put together any kind of business or foundation or whatever you wanted . . . You have a lot of energy to work with . . . You're probably not very lazy . . . If anything, you should relax a lot more . . . This Aries Midheaven may seem to be in sharp contrast to all your Aquarius and Pisces influences . . . And it is . . . It provides a very good balance . . . Aries is the beginning of all signs — a symbol of rebirth . . . of creative energy . . .

. . . with
Uranus in
Aries in 10th
house

This is further highlighted by Uranus in Aries in your 10th house . . . Uranus is a symbol of the energy of your 7th chakra, the 'crown chakra', the 'opening of Brahma' — the place at which we actually can connect with the whole Universe, and experience the one . . . Uranus rules Aquarius . . . and it is always associated with explosive change, with movement, with discovery . . . and with shattering old rigid models of behavior . . .

Your work in the world, and your 'career' in general, is bound to blow some people's minds

118

... and it's bound to be creative, and ever-changing, in some ways.

Taurus is the Fixed or Sustaining Earth sign, a sign of stability and groundedness ... it often points to strength and persistance and focus... The 11th house is the natural house of Aquarius, and it is associated with the areas of things which go beyond the 10th house physical plane activity: ideals, visions, dreams, fantasy, prayer, the spirit of Oneness of all humankind ... also innovation and new discoveries... With Taurus ruling here, you have another strong Aquarian influence ... go with the flow of your own natural energies...

Taurus rules 11th house...

Your Part of Fortune is here, too: Fortune is a Gypsy mark, which is said to show where your *true* fortune lies (your true satisfaction in life, beyond your career and work of your 10th house...) — so your true fortune, too, is to be found in your ideals, your visions, your imagination... And though your Fortune is in the 11th house, it is in the sign of Gemini — the Communicator... This points to teaching again ... and writing... You are a channel of clear information for friends and students...

... with Fortune in Gemini...

This is made even more powerful and deeper with Gemini ruling your 12th house... It is difficult to say much about the 12th house, because, like Pluto, it goes beyond the realm of words ... for it is a symbol of that which goes beyond even our visions, dreams, prayers of the 11th house ... it is a symbol of the Beyond ... the Absolute ... total perfection ... the Ultimate ... God ... the Universe...

Gemini rules 12th house...

119

... with Pluto on the Ascendant
You have something to communicate about these realms ...

... something totally beyond words ...

OM

In Conclusion

Follow me on a short meditation:

The Kabbala — Jewish mysticism — gives many deep teachings... Here is one of the finest I have found*... It can place all of astrology, in fact any means of growth or way of life, into a beautiful perspective...

The Kabbala is the study of the Tree of Life, with its 10 stages, or 'sephiroth'... The Tree of Life can explain a great deal, if you have ears to hear — the creation of the Universe, the nature of mind, the nature of reality...

(Follow as much of this journey as you wish, and let the rest go ... the only important part is the *end*...)

The Kabbala says that in the beginning was the vast void, the number zero, shining pure infinity...

Then, the One appeared — a point of focus within this infinite space... This is the first Sephiroth, the Crown...

O

Then, the essence of the miracle of creation occurs, the most wondrous thing in the Universe: the One becomes the Two... The second and third Sephiroth, the Father and Mother, appear.

O

O   **O**

---

* Much of this information comes from Israel Regardie — from *The Tree of Life*, and other books. Deep thanks to him for his work.

All this takes place on the highest spiritual levels, in very high, subtle forms, beyond our words of description . . .

Then, this creative urge is reflected to a denser level, the level of thought . . . Creation becomes a thought . . . And there are six Sephiroth . . .

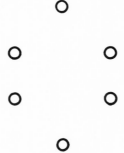

Then, it is reflected to a still denser level, the emotional level . . . Creation becomes a feeling, a desire . . . The astral realms are born . . . And there are nine Sephiroth . . .

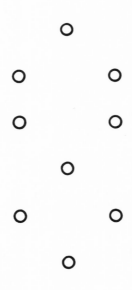

Then, the material plane becomes manifest... The physical plane which we can see, touch, feel... The 10th Sephiroth is born...

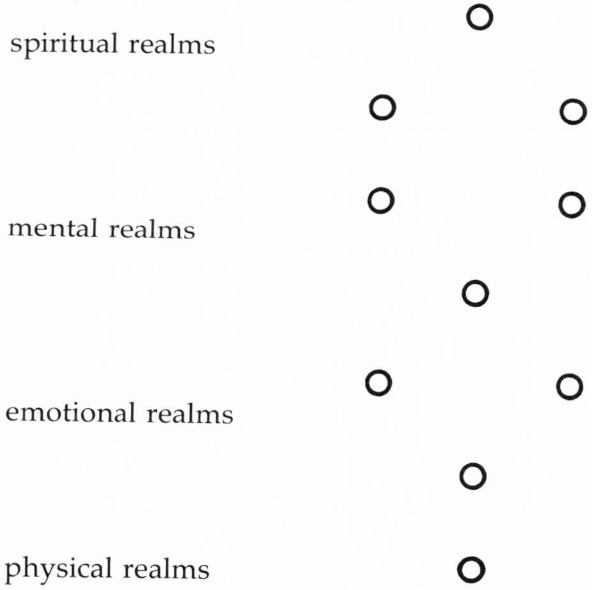

spiritual realms

mental realms

emotional realms

physical realms

This shows us that everything we create, including our own bodies and every other created thing, is first a spritual impulse, then a mental impulse, a thought, then an emotional impulse, a feeling — and then it becomes manifest on the material plane for all to see and feel... Now we're coming to the end of our journey into creation...

There is one planetary symbol which embraces this entire journey ... one symbol which connects and unifies the whole Tree of Life...

One planet which goes beyond all . . .

One planet, one energy, one power, which symbolizes the force of creation, which is the force of God . . . the key to the mysteries . . .

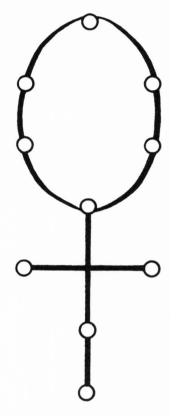

It is Venus, the power of Love.

"*The end of all wisdom is love, love, love.*"
—Sai Baba

"*A new law I give to you:*
Love one another,
as I have loved you . . ."
—A prophet and teacher
named Jesus

At the Threshold

Wherever we wander,
  I will call you my friend
No distance between us
  Nothing to defend
Break all barriers down
  We have bridges to mend
And a love to lighten our laughter
  and a love to grow everafter . . .

Sisters and brothers
  We will call all humankind
Wherever we wander
  Our heart-friends we will find
A New Age of Light is born
  An old dark age is dying
With a love that frees us from past karma
  A new light, a new law, a new dharma

  Be in peace . . .
    Be in peace . . .

In our hearts
  a new age is born
And we stand
  at the threshold of morn!

— from *Seeds to the Wind*
by Marcus Allen

125

About the Author

I encourage every astrologer to include his or her chart with any books or articles they write about astrology. It really helps to see where the astrologer is coming from, and going to . . . Here's my chart — by now, it will give you a lot of information about me:

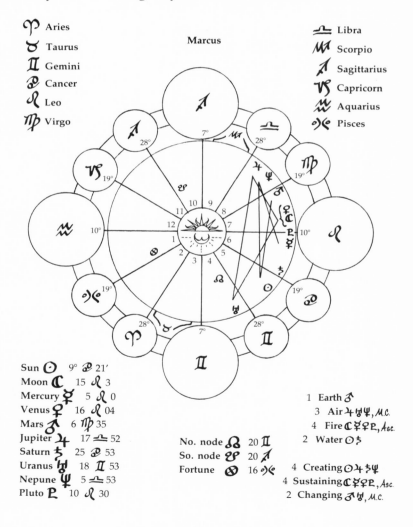

♈	Aries	♎	Libra
♉	Taurus	♏	Scorpio
♊	Gemini	♐	Sagittarius
♋	Cancer	♑	Capricorn
♌	Leo	♒	Aquarius
♍	Virgo	♓	Pisces

Marcus

Sun ☉	9° ♋ 21′
Moon ☽	15 ♌ 3
Mercury ☿	5 ♌ 0
Venus ♀	16 ♌ 04
Mars ♂	6 ♍ 35
Jupiter ♃	17 ♎ 52
Saturn ♄	25 ♋ 53
Uranus ♅	18 ♊ 53
Nepune ♆	5 ♎ 53
Pluto ♇	10 ♌ 30

No. node ☊ 20 ♊
So. node ☋ 20 ♐
Fortune ⊗ 16 ♓

1 Earth ♂
3 Air ♃ ♅ ♆, M.C.
4 Fire ☽ ☿ ♀ ♇, Asc.
2 Water ☉ ♄

4 Creating ☉ ♃ ♄ ♆
4 Sustaining ☽ ☿ ♀ ♇, Asc.
2 Changing ♂ ♅, M.C.

Be in Peace